# Ferdinand of Brunswick, Minden & the Seven Year's War

# Ferdinand of Brunswick, Minden & the Seven Year's War
## ILLUSTRATED

Minden and the Seven Years' War

Sir Lees Knowles

An Account of the Battle of Vellinghausen & A Short Historical account of The Battle of Minden
by Charles Townshend
&
James Grant

LEONAUR

*Ferdinand of Brunswick, Minden & the Seven Year's War*
ILLUSTRATED
*Minden and the Seven Years' War*
By Sir Lees Knowles
*An Account of the Battle of Vellinghausen &*
*A Short Historical account of The Battle of Minden*
by Charles Townshend
&
James Grant

FIRST EDITION

Leonaur is an imprint of Oakpast Ltd
Copyright in this form © 2017 Oakpast Ltd

ISBN: 978-1-78282-608-8 (hardcover)
ISBN: 978-1-78282-609-5 (softcover)

http://www.leonaur.com

Publisher's Notes

The views expressed in this book are not necessarily those of the publisher.

# Contents

| | |
|---|---|
| The Seven Years' War | 7 |
| Combined Naval and Military Expeditions, 1757-1758 | 13 |
| Minden: 1759 | 18 |
| The Battle of Minden | 23 |
| Minden, and After | 38 |
| The Campaign of 1760: Warburg | 42 |
| Vellinghausen: 1761 | 53 |
| Wilhelmsthal and Amöneburg: 1762 | 59 |
| Peace | 65 |
| General-Field-Marshal Ferdinand, Prince of Brunswick and Lüneburg | 70 |
| The Hereditary Prince, Afterwards, the Duke of Brunswick | 77 |
| The Minden Regiments | 82 |
| The Charge Against Lord George Sackville | 101 |
| Vellinghausen | 111 |
| Minden, 1759 | 135 |

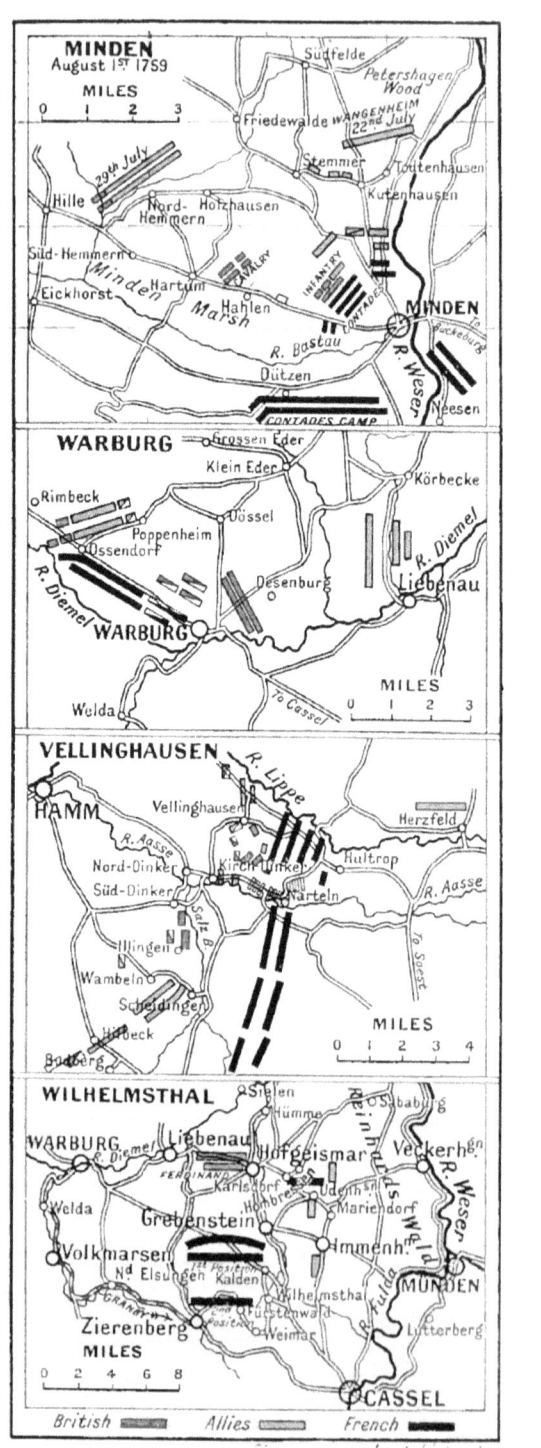

Chapter 1

# The Seven Years' War

The Seven Years' War with its struggle between the powers of Europe cannot be appreciated without a review of the chief events which preceded it.

The treaty of Aix-la-Chapelle, possessing no lasting qualities, brought about a merely temporary settlement of the existing troubles. Its terms were ambiguous and vague, and they satisfied none of the signatory Powers. Moreover, it left the boundaries in America as a source of irritation between England and France. The Empress Maria Theresa regarded Austria as the victim of spoliation, so long as Frederick the Great was allowed to keep possession of the Province of Silesia, the fact that that Province had been ceded by treaty making no difference to her. Guided by the far-seeing Kaunitz, her Imperial Chancellor, the Empress decided to renounce the traditional policy of the Hapsburgs, to abandon treaties and friendship with England, and to enter into an alliance with France.

An alliance between the House of Bourbon, representing France, and the House of Hapsburg-Lorraine, representing Austria, had been regarded hitherto as an impossibility. But, the old order was now changed, and France was drawn by Austria slowly but surely, with a persevering subtilty of purpose, into a net which bound her down by the Treaty of Versailles. Thus, there became united the two traditional enemies, France and Austria.

The extent of the reversal of policy can be appreciated from the fact that France was still an ally of Prussia, and that Frederick the Great, the King of Prussia, was personally upon the worst terms with his Uncle, King George the Second of England. In fact, the subsequent invasion of the Dominions of Hanover through Westphalia was adopted by France upon the advice given by Frederick to the French

Ambassador in Berlin.

The Empress Maria Theresa had worked for some years assiduously and secretly for the creation of a league between Austria, France, Russia, Saxony and Sweden, with the object of destroying the King of Prussia, "the common enemy", or "the Solomon of the North", as Voltaire called him, and of making a partition of his kingdom. It was proposed to give each of the conquering powers a province, or a slice of territory.

But, trifles often produce great results, and so it happened. Frederick the Great had given mortal offence to three prominent women who were able to wield great power. First, by a scathing epigram, he brought upon himself the savage enmity of Elizabeth, Czarina of Russia. Secondly, he fell foul of Madame de Pompadour, Mistress of Louis XV, "*le Bien Aimé*," King of France. She was courted by the representatives of every Power in Europe, with the exception of Prussia: even the Duke of Newcastle, England's chief Minister of State, exchanged dainty notes and presents with her. But Frederick, by the contemptuous remark "I don't know her", in response to friendly overtures, won from her relentless hostility. And thirdly, he offended the Empress Maria Theresa.

These three women who, in their secret correspondence, addressed one another in terms of cousinly affection, were, in their private lives, as far apart as the poles. Now, however, they were bound together for the purpose of revenge, into a compact and indissoluble coalition. Frederick the Great was their enemy. War was inevitable. Their cockpit was Europe.

To appreciate still further the complex situation, it is necessary to give some outline of English motives, policy and action. Between England and France war became certain, when, in April, 1754, the Virginian local troops under George Washington were defeated at Fort Duquesne on the Ohio. In consequence of that defeat, an Expedition under Admiral Keppel and General Braddock was sent out by England in defence of her Territory in America.

At the end of January, 1755, the English Cabinet decided to send a Squadron to North America in order to prevent French ships from landing troops in Nova Scotia or Cape Breton, and from passing through the St. Lawrence to Quebec. Admiral Boscawen was appointed to command, and he sailed on April 21st, 1755, with instructions to fall upon any ships having on board troops or munitions of war. This was a secret blow, such as nations formerly dealt one another when any advantage was to be gained. The French Ambassador was assured that no warlike instructions had been given.

In June, Admiral Boscawen fell in with a French squadron, gave chase to it, and captured three vessels. As soon as the news of that event reached Paris, Mirepoix, the French Ambassador, was recalled from London; but, beyond making vain threats, the French remained passive, for the Government of Louis XV was conspicuous for its apathy and irresolution. It is, however, indisputable that they desired peace with England. Mirepoix was earnest in his efforts to maintain peace; but, the matters in dispute between England and France were too important to be settled without the arbitrament of war.

Admiral A. T. Mahan, of the United States Navy, the author of *The Influence of Sea-power on History*, gives details of the peculiar nonintervention on the part of the French Government. For instance, Admiral Boscawen lay in wait for the French convoy at the mouth of the St. Lawrence. In July, 1755, Sir Edward Hawke was sent to sea with orders to cruise off Ushant and Cape Finisterre, and to seize any ships of the line he might see. In August, further orders were added, to take all French ships of every kind, men-of-war, privateers, and merchantmen, and to send them into English ports. Before the end of the year, 300 trading-vessels, valued at 6,000,000 dollars, or about one and a quarter million pounds sterling, had been captured, and 6,000 French seamen, enough to man nearly ten ships of the line, were imprisoned in England. All this occurred, tolerated by the French, while nominal peace still existed. War was not declared until six months later.

King George the Second possessed one cardinal impelling thought, the security and defence of his territory of Hanover. If the king had not been the Elector, Hanover would have had but little concern for the Government of England, although it is more than probable that the course of events would have forced the country into an alliance with Frederick. The Duke of Newcastle, a despicable politician in English history, was ready to adopt any policy that would ensure the support of the king, and a continuance of power for himself. The Duke of Cumberland and his party clamoured for a settlement by force. The people wanted a war with France, chiefly on account of their hatred of the Bourbons; but, they preferred a Maritime and Colonial, to a Continental, war.

In September, 1755, a convention was signed between England and Russia. The knowledge of this convention, and of a secret understanding between France and Austria, completed the isolation of

Prussia, and forced Frederick into the arms of England.

In April, 1756, Port Mahon in Minorca, which for fifty years had belonged to England, capitulated to the French, and the failure to relieve it of Admiral Byng, who for his failure was tried, and, on March 14th, 1757, shot, brought a crisis to a head. Byng shirked from hatred of responsibility, though not personally a coward: he was the scapegoat of the Duke of Newcastle, and William Pitt tried in vain to save him. When it was known that the French were in Minorca, England declared war.

The Seven Years' War, so far as England is concerned, may be divided into two phases, namely, the Colonial and Maritime, and the Continental. As soon as William Pitt became the Minister for War, and the real head of the Government, the struggle resolved itself into one for the supremacy of the seas, and whether England or France should be the chief imperial power. King George assured Parliament that vigorous support would be given to the promotion of British pretensions in America, and a special grant of one million pounds was voted promptly with that object in view.

This was the era of secret treaties. The powers were re-arranging themselves for warfare which might flare up at any moment, the duration of which no man could foresee, and old alliances were broken.

England was bound to Hanover by the tie that George the Second, King of England, was the Elector of Hanover. Prussia, a powerful neighbour, might be a dangerous enemy; but, Prussia, as a friend, might save Hanover from the attacks of other powers. The King of Prussia knew too well that England was his only possible ally, and he suggested between Prussia and England "a neutrality convention", which in effect was an agreement to attack jointly any non-German armed-force setting foot on German soil, the Austria-Netherlands excepted.

As a preliminary, England paid twenty thousand pounds for the damage done during the previous war to Prussian shipping, and Prussia paid the balance of the Silesian loan.

The convention signed at Westminster on January 16th, 1756, came as a great surprise to the Diplomatic world, proclaiming as it did a complete change in the existing armed combinations. It was followed by the treaty of Versailles, secretly negotiated by the astute Kaunitz so long previously as 1753, by which France and Austria were bound together for the coming struggle.

England had for some months been negotiating with, and bribing, the *Czarina*. The subsidy-treaty thus secured had been scarcely ratified, when the Russian sovereign discovered the existence of the Convention between England and Prussia, and, full of anger, she withdrew at once from her engagement. Perfidy does not appear to be too strong a term in describing England's treatment of Russia; for, England was bound by treaty to confide to her any steps that should be taken to come to an understanding with the "common enemy". This diplomacy was characteristic of the times.

Frederick the Great, familiarly known, later, as "old Fritz" (*der alte Fritz*), had now complete proof of the conspiracy which had been formed against him. He had been warned,—and he saw the war-clouds gathering—,that the moment had come when he should bring matters to a head. Peremptorily, he demanded from the Empress Maria Theresa an explanation of certain threatening circumstances, and in curt terms he was refused a reply. Without the loss of a day, with sixty thousand men, he invaded Saxony, and that invasion was the real Continental beginning of the Seven Years' War.

The Prussian Army marched in three columns, with intervals of 50 miles between each, which reached simultaneously their appointed positions in Saxony on September 9th, 1756. It had never been in a more perfect, or in a higher, state of efficiency than when Frederick the Great led it into Saxony, setting a personal example of bravery for his men. On one occasion, when some soldiers hesitated to attack the enemy, he asked them the question, "do you wish to live for ever?" "*Wollt ihr immer leben?*" Moreover, Frederick recognised the aristocracy of intellect. On one occasion, the Court Chamberlain remonstrated with him for admitting Voltaire to his own table, though men of high rank were compelled to sit at another. Frederick replied, "privileged persons rank equal with kings".

The English Army at this time was a bye-word. Hessians and Hanoverians were hired and brought over to England to defend the Country against the threatened invasion of France. Such was its condition under the government, that regiments were without colonels; because, if they were appointed by the Duke of Cumberland, they would be hostile to the Party and interests of that old intriguer, the Duke of Newcastle. Generals were nominated to active command on the qualifying merit that they had reached a ripe old age.

One of the ablest, and perhaps one of the most unscrupulous, politicians of the day, said of the government; about to enter into war with France, that "they were no more able to direct this war than his three children". However, in the history of nations, the man has been found for every crisis, and in this crisis England produced one of her greatest sons, William Pitt.

When his hour came, Pitt announced the supreme task of his life in words which, on his lips, were no vainglorious boast:

> I know that I can save this country, and that no one else can.

And so, England was saved.

Chapter 2

# Combined Naval and Military Expeditions, 1757-1758

After the short duration and failure of the Pitt-Devonshire Administration, the Government of the day was entrusted to William Pitt under the nominal leadership of the Duke of Newcastle, and, in allusion to this combination, Horace Walpole said, "Mr. Pitt does everything, the Duke of Newcastle gives everything."

William Pitt, a man of lofty ideals and indomitable will, was now not only in office but also in power. His ideals were based on the promotion of British Commerce, and everything that is contained in the expression "sea-power", in other words, the sole object of Pitt was the supremacy of the British at sea. He devised a combination of the sea and land forces, and, in his first experiment with this new power, he had the good fortune or ability to discover two officers who were in themselves the embodiment of the best traditions of their respective services, namely, Howe and Wolfe. The best illustration of such a combination may be given in the co-operation of Admiral Saunders and General Wolfe at Quebec. Wolfe, when he was given by Pitt the command of the expedition to Canada, was only thirty-two years old.

In this connection, it is of interest to quote the view of the relations of the army to Parliament, as expressed by Pitt in the House of Commons on November 4th, 1745:

> The right of inquiring what measures may conduce to the advantage and security of the public belongs, not to the army, but to this House; to this House belongs the power of constituting the army, or of advising His Majesty with regard to its constitution; our armies have no better right to determine for them-

George II

selves than any other body of men; nor are we to suffer them to prescribe laws to the Legislature, or to govern those by whose authority they subsist.

In the two years 1757-1758, Pitt sent against the coast of France three expeditions, which at the time were scoffed at by incompetent generals and unprofessional soldiers, men who, unable to see beyond the limited horizon of their immediate surroundings, were not ashamed to leave the shores of England with failure in their hearts.

"Make descents on the naked coast of France and spread alarm the whole length of Brittany and Normandy" was the advice urged again and again upon the British Government by Frederick the Great, and the value of this policy was shown by its result. When Austria, under an agreement, demanded from France 24,000 men, France demurred, saying that she had "to keep them on the waste of the ocean". In fact, at one time there were four camps of 80,000 men at Calais, Havre, Brest, Rochefort and La Rochelle.

Pitt did not expect, or wish, to retain any French territory in Europe; but, he knew from the experience of his own countrymen at home how demoralising is the fear of invasion. He wished to humiliate the French and to make the European Powers feel the supremacy of the British at sea, and so he determined to ruin the French fleets, and the naval bases upon which they depended.

The first expedition left England in 1757, under the command of General Sir John Mordaunt, and its objective was Rochefort. The generals, before they had reached their destination, suggested that the expedition should return to England; but, the admiral, Sir Edward Hawke, refused to consent, and it was with difficulty that they prevailed upon him to assemble a Council of War. It is sufficient to say that the expedition failed and that Sir John Mordaunt, was tried by court martial, and acquitted. Colonel Wolfe, who held the position of quartermaster-general, was of opinion that the admiral was too cautious, and that there was unnecessary delay. He had gone ashore and reconnoitred, and advised "a quick and resolute stroke." Subsequently, he wrote:

> That afternoon and night there slipped through our hands the lucky moment of surprise, and consternation among our enemies.

The second expedition left England in May, 1758: this was against St. Malo. The command of the land-forces was entrusted to the Duke of Marlborough, the Master-General of the Ordnance, the bearer of a great name, but a man of poor ability. Moreover, he was dominated completely by his second-in-command, Lord George Sackville. At St. Servan, they burned shipping to the value of three-quarters of a million pounds. When, however, they learned that the French were advancing upon them, fearing that they might be cut off from the sea, they made a hurried embarkation. The correctness of this withdrawal has not been justified, and the military character of Sackville cast a shadow over the Expedition, which proved both expensive and abortive. From Horace Walpole, we know that the troops openly questioned his capacity, and that Howe, usually solid and silent as a rock, conceived and expressed an extreme aversion to him. The fleet was kept in Cancale Bay for a week, when it visited Havre and Cherbourg, and returned early in July to Spithead.

Taking advantage of the warlike enthusiasm aroused by the victory of Prince Ferdinand at Crefeld, Pitt decided to reinforce the Prince's army by a British contingent, and Lieutenant-General Bligh was nominated to command. Such was the news which reached the fleet on its arrival at Spithead. The Duke of Marlborough and Lord George Sackville left at once for London, and, by using interest and influence in high places, they were appointed to the command of the division under orders for service in Germany, and yet Sackville had declared publicly that he had had "enough of buccaneering expeditions." So, when General Bligh arrived in London from Ireland, he found that he was to take up the command that Marlborough had vacated, and the duty that the latter had shirked.

The third expedition against the coast of France sailed on August 1st, 1758. The squadron was commanded by Commodore Howe. On August 6th, Howe bombarded Cherbourg, and on the following day he sailed to Sainte-Marie's Bay. Troops were landed and attacked Cherbourg, which surrendered after a feeble resistance. The docks, the defences of the city, and the shipping were destroyed. The troops remained for more than a week in the town, where they were guilty of every excess, and General Bligh was unable to keep them in check. Then, they re-embarked, and, after some delay, owing to adverse winds, the fleet sailed to the Bay of St. Lunaire, twelve miles to the west of St. Malo, where they were landed again with the object of attacking that town. It became necessary for the fleet to change its anchorage, and this caused the general to order a march over land to St. Cast. Mismanagement and incapacity were shown by General Bligh in the conduct of this retreat, which resulted in a disastrous embarkation, and the loss of 700 officers and men. Thus, ended ingloriously the third expedition of Pitt against the French coast.

On the Continent, events were proceeding rapidly. In July, 1767, the Duke of Cumberland was defeated at Hastenbeck, and, on September 8th, signed the Convention of Kloster (Cloister, or Convent) Zeven, by which his army of 30,000 Hanoverians and Hessians laid down their arms, and were broken up as a force, without becoming prisoners of war.

George the Second disclaimed this convention, and threw the blame and responsibility for it on his son, the duke. When the duke came into the royal presence, the king did not address him, but said aloud "here is my son, who has ruined me and disgraced himself." The duke resigned his appointments and retired from active life. Pitt took the side of the duke, and when the king once said that he had given no orders for such a convention to be signed, he answered, "but full powers, sir,—very full powers". It was proved to be so: for, a letter from the king to the duke is extant, in which His Majesty says, "I trust my affairs (in Germany) entirely to your conduct."

Pitt had almost a feudal respect for the sovereign: it was this that influenced him greatly, when he accepted the Hanoverian policy of the king. He was an Imperialist, and yet a democratic statesman. He was called the Great Commoner, just as Frederick was called the Great Emperor: but, the greatness of Pitt came from the people. He was a nation-maker, and an empire-builder.

George the Second was induced by Pitt to place Prince Ferdinand of Brunswick at the head of the Hanoverian army of 30,000 men. This bold and capable General soon drove the French from the electorate, making one flank secure for the much oppressed Frederick. He followed up his success by forcing the French over the Rhine, and by gaining a crushing victory over them at Crefeld. Pitt was now becoming daily a firmer ally. Suddenly, he determined to reinforce the army of Prince Ferdinand by a British Division, and, within two weeks, 7,000 men under the Duke of Marlborough were landed at Emden, on August 21st, 1758, joining Ferdinand's army at Crefeld. The Duke of Marlborough died on or about August 20th, and he was succeeded in the command by Lord George Sackville. The allies at this time effected nothing of importance, and, at the end of November, the British went into winter-quarters in the City of Münster, and in the towns of Rheims and Steinort.

CHAPTER 3

# Minden: 1759

The year 1759, the most glorious probably that England has ever seen, the year in which William Pitt the younger was born, opened with gloomy prospects for the Anglo-German allies, and especially for Frederick. The Battle of Zorndorf fought on August 25th, 1758, was one of the most sanguinary battles of the age, and it was waged with peculiar hatred and ferocity. The Russian casualties numbered 21,000, including 8,000 killed. The marauding Cossacks, who devastated the country with incendiary fires in all directions, were deemed to be past forgiveness. Their extermination was the only remedy in the opinion of their foes. "Not a devil of you shall escape," said the Prussian Hussars as they surrounded a burning barn, in which they had trapped 400 Cossacks.

The Battle of Hochkirchen was fought on October 14th, 1758, the eleventh general action fought in two years. From this battle, Frederick, with consummate mastery, extricated his army from a serious defeat. Surprised before dawn, he found himself surrounded, and the enemy in his camp. Fighting hand to hand, he withdrew his troops from the meshes which had been woven around them, and, deceiving his opponent by skilful manoeuvres, he gained a strategical victory by throwing his army across the direct road to Silesia.

Frederick spent the winter of 1758-9 in Breslau. He was full of sorrows, he wrote:

If my head were a fountain of tears, it would not suffice for the grief I feel.

At this time, he had one solace, the vigorous application required in steady and continuous labour. He worked without ceasing to improve his army, and to supervise the most minute affairs of State. One important innovation should be noticed: he introduced horse-artillery into the Prussian service, and in the subsequent campaign of 1759, field-guns drawn rapidly by teams of horses, with soldiers mounted as outriders, were brought into action for the first time. This idea was considered a brilliant one, and it was imitated quickly by the Austrian and by the other armies.

In two years neither side could claim that in the aggregate it had gained any material advantage. Frederick had but one hope, and that was peace. He calculated upon one supreme and final struggle, and then peace. But, the pride and vindictive hatred of three women had yet to be appeased. To them, a few reverses, even defeats, were of no moment, but merely incidents of war. They evolved fresh plans, and made more determined efforts, to strike down the king who had treated them, one by one, with more or less contempt. And so, five nations were pitted against one, and that one had for its chief military asset the king, who during the next four years established amongst his contemporaries the reputation which has been confirmed by the verdict of posterity.

The new year 1759 opened with the allied army at Fulda under Prince Ferdinand of Brunswick. The British contingent of about 12,000 men was under the command of Lord George Sackville. Until the middle of April, there were only a few minor operations, including an unsuccessful attack made by Ferdinand upon the French at Bergen near Frankfurt, in which British soldiers were not engaged.

On May 18th, the prince moved his headquarters to Lippstadt; on June 3rd the British infantry left their cantonments and encamped near Luynan, and on June 11th the whole allied army was assembled in the neighbourhood of Werl and Soest. In this month, the grenadier companies, one from each of the British regiments, were formed into one battalion, of which the command was conferred upon Major Maxwell of Kingsley's Regiment. This officer was of gigantic stature and proportions. In a private letter, Wolfe, when lieutenant-colonel, asked his friends at Bath to look out for Bardolf (Major Maxwell), who, he said, would be found probably in the ballrooms. In battle, he was a hero, and, in the drawing-room, he was a courtier.

On June 16th, the rival armies were in sight of each other at Lichtenau, and, four days later, after various changes, they were in camp near Reitburg, the right flank of the allies being covered by the corps of General von Wangenheim, who remained at Duelmen in the district of Münster.

On June 30th, after moves and countermoves on the part of the opposing forces, the allies were encamped between Marienfeld and the village of Harsewinkel. As these movements developed, the French marshal, Contades, showed an intention to cut off the allies from their supplies at Osnabrück, and to drive a wedge in between them and the River Weser. In order to defeat this intention, on July 3rd, Ferdinand concentrated his army at Dissen, General Wangenheim occupying Cadbergen. The light troops were at Halle in advance of the main body. The French marshals, de Broglie and Contades, made a counter demonstration, the former moving to Heepen, while the latter took possession of Bielefeld and Herford.

It was now a race between the contending armies for the town of Minden, and the passage of the Weser. The French seized Halle, driving out the allied light troops, and in turn they were driven out by the British grenadiers and dragoons. Marshal de Broglie was now close upon Minden, his corps stretching along the left bank of the Weser, and holding all the roads and approaches leading to the- town, while Marshal Contades was at Bielefeld, within striking distance, and in a position to give support with an effective force, if necessary.

On July 8th, Prince Ferdinand fell back upon Osnabrück, his retirement being covered by the hereditary prince, his nephew, Charles William Ferdinand of Brunswick. The same evening, Marshal de Broglie marched from Enger to Minden at the head of sixteen Battalions, together with detachments fourteen hundred strong and four regiments of cavalry, and, at daybreak on July 9th, he appeared before the town, and summoned it to surrender. Major-General Zastrow refused to relinquish his trust, saying "I have guns, powder, and soldiers; and, before I can think of capitulation, all these must first have vanished", and the town was at once invested.

The first intention of Broglie was to take Minden by assault, but the point of weakness was on the other side of the Weser, and he had neither boats nor pontoons with which to effect the passage of the river. However, a float of timber was found by a reconnoitring party, and, by means of this raft, Fischer's corps, and three hundred volunteers, were enabled to cross and take the entrenchments at the head of the bridge. According to German contemporary accounts and tradition, the French were helped by the treachery of a peasant. Broglie covered the attack by a heavy cannonade. The French forced an entrance successfully, and, by 9 o'clock in the evening of July 9th, they were masters of the town of Minden.

The garrison to the number of about fifteen hundred, consisting of a Hessian Battalion and detachments of other corps, were taken prisoners, together with Major-General Zastrow.

The importance of Minden to the French was, that it secured the passage of the Weser, with an open road to Hanover, and, that it contained a magazine of stores.

On July 10th, Marshal Contades moved from Bielefeld to Herford. On the same day, Prince Ferdinand heard of the capture of Minden, and he pushed forward at once a division of 10,000 men under the hereditary prince, to secure the position of Stolzenau on the Weser. The light troops of this division commanded by Colonel Fredericks fell in with a party of 500 French Infantry between Diepenau and Stolzenau, and, attacking them, killed and wounded a considerable number, and made 200 prisoners. Next, they came into conflict with a body of cavalry 600 strong, which Colonel Fredericks ordered the Prussian Hussars to attack in front, while he cut off their retreat. Thus, 200 Frenchmen were killed, and the remainder, with their commanding-officer, Count de Solles, were made prisoners.

Prince Ferdinand moved by rapid marches to Stolzenau, where he arrived on July 14th. His immediate object was to prevent a junction of the forces of Marshals Contades and Broglie, and he made, therefore, a night march to Petershagen Heath, on July 16th; but, on that day Contades had reached Minden, and Broglie, having passed the Weser, was holding the road to Bückeburg.

The French had chosen a position too strong for attack with any prospect of success. They were posted behind the Minden morass, through which runs the brook Bastau, their right resting on the town, and their left touching the mountain-village of Hartenhausen.

Wangenheim advanced with his division to the Plain of Minden where, on July 17th, he occupied the villages of Todtenhausen, Kutenhausen, and Stemmer. The main portion of the army followed; but, as the enemy changed their dispositions, Frederick ordered a return to the camp at Petershagen. On July 22nd, Wangenheim was again in position on the plain, close to the village of Todtenhausen, with his left flank touching the Weser.

On July 27th, the hereditary prince marched with 6,000 men to Lübbecke, and drove from it a body of French troops stationed there for the protection of the left flank of Marshal Contades. On the same day, General Dreve recaptured Osnabrück, and then joined the hereditary prince, when the combined force marched to Herford, and, on

July 31st, captured a position at Kirchlengern, which lay in the direct path of the enemy's convoys with supplies from Cassel.

The last general change of the position of the allied forces was made on July 29th, when Ferdinand lead the remainder of his army in three columns from Petershagen to Hille, holding the line from Hille to Friedewalde. The British held the post of honour on the right, and the headquarters of Ferdinand at Hille were guarded by the Regiments of Napier and Kingsley, the 12th and 20th, respectively. The British piquets held the village of Hartum, the Hanoverians were in Südhemmern and the Brunswickers in Stemmer: to the Hessians and cavalry piquets was committed the care of the wood between Hartum and Holzhausen, and cavalry-detachments held the road between Hartum and Hahlen. About 2,000 men were sent to Lübbecke, to maintain communication with the hereditary prince.

Ferdinand on July 31st, for the second time, enjoined upon his general-officers the necessity of making themselves acquainted with the routes which their columns were to take in marching to the plain of Minden, and he pressed upon them the necessity of examining carefully the ground between the windmill of Hahlen, and the village of Stemmer.

It appeared as if Ferdinand knew exactly the intention of the French, and the following is the story told of how he obtained his information. Contades, on July 29th, asked the mayor of Minden for a reliable man as a messenger. A man was chosen who happened to have been a sailor and to have learnt French and English. Contades thought that he was a Westphalian who spoke only the local dialect, and he addressed him through an interpreter. He ordered him to take a pair of shoes to the Duke of Brissac at Herford, and to obtain 2,000 pairs like them, for his soldiers. The peasant, however, overheard that the shoes contained despatches. He started on his errand: but, instead of going to Herford direct, he hurried across the marsh to Hille, and enabled Ferdinand to read the despatches of Contades, before taking the shoes to the Duke of Brissac.

CHAPTER 4

# The Battle of Minden

The French marshal, Contades, held a position that could not be assailed with any prospect of success. He was stronger in men than Ferdinand, whom he could have worn out by inactivity, had his communications with his base at Cassel been secure: but, to keep open seventy miles of road, with an active and enterprising enemy, was both a disquieting and a difficult task. He knew that a force of 6,000 men lay across the path by which his supplies must travel, and this gave an impetus to his desire to bring matters to a conclusion. The advantages which he had gained up till now were neutralised by the ever-present fear that his line of communication would be cut off.

At this moment, the position of Ferdinand seemed to Contades to invite attack and destruction. The corps of General von Wangenheim was isolated on the plain of Minden, and, with one flank, as it were, in mid-air, it appeared to indicate incomprehensible weakness, offering to Contades an opportunity for which he could scarcely have hoped from an able antagonist. The plan of battle was so simple as to permit of no doubt of success: it was, first, to crush the unsupported Wangenheim, and then to turn on the unprotected flank of Ferdinand, driving a living-wedge into the gap of three miles which separated them.

There were other inducements to make a prompt and supreme effort: for instance, the detaching of the hereditary prince's corps of 6,000 men, the weakening of the main body which was already inferior in numbers to the French, and the scattering of fragments of the Allies among the villages and hamlets of the plain, which constituted a provocation almost insolent in its rashness. Contades was led into temptation, and he fell. Ferdinand had purposely conveyed the impression of heedlessness, and of insecurity, to the mind of Contades, so as to tempt him to leave his stronghold and come out into the open.

Tuesday, July 31st, was spent by the French Army in building eight bridges over the Bastau. Marshal de Broglie was ordered to cross the Weser by the town-bridge, and then the 51,000 men, with 162 guns, in nine columns, were to march to their places in the line of battle.

Wednesday, August 1st, 1759, was ushered in by the French Army moving to the eight bridges on the Bastau River. There is some doubt as to the actual number of the bridges which the French threw across the river. Carlyle says nineteen, apparently following the German accounts; but, Fortescue, in his monumental *History of the Army*, gives the number as eight. There was marked confusion and absence of discipline on the part of both officers and men. The eight columns were two hours behind their time. Broglie was in his position with precise punctuality; but, the absence of the eight columns compelled him to remain inactive, when he should have been attacking Wangenheim. This was a piece of good fortune for Ferdinand.

Two deserters from the French Army were brought in by the piquets to the Prince of Anhalt, the general-officer of the day, with the important intelligence that the whole Army was in motion. Ferdinand had observed, during the previous evening, signs of an unusual stir, and he gave instructions that he was to be informed of the slightest movement; but, through the carelessness of the Prince of Anhalt, the valuable intelligence of the deserters was not sent to him for two hours.

The instructions of Ferdinand were clear and concise. They had been issued the previous day. The cavalry had been ordered to be saddled at one o'clock in the morning. At three o'clock, Ferdinand called the whole army to arms, and ordered them to march to their appointed positions. The advance in eight columns was to be made by five o'clock, but it was seven o'clock before they were in position. All were then ranked in order of battle, except the cavalry of the right, where there was complete confusion. The general in command, Lord George Sackville, although he had received precise instructions, could not be found. He should have been at the village of Hahlen, on which the allied right was to rest, to prevent the French from occupying it. The piquets from Hartum were sent to Hahlen, only to find the French in position.

Ferdinand was everywhere. He was the imposing figure of the battle. Sometimes with only a solitary *aide-de-camp*, and at other times with only a groom, he galloped from one important point to another. His anxieties were great. The stupidity of one general, and the disloy-

Marquis of Granby

alty and disobedience of another, had imperilled his plan of action and the safety of his army. Wangenheim at Todtenhausen, and the piquets at Hille, were engaged simultaneously. The French had six guns on the causeway of Eickhorst which led through the morass, which is now reclaimed and cultivated, to Hille. Ferdinand had posted 500 men and two guns to seal this point, and although he felt that it was only a demonstration, he ordered General Gilfoe from Lübbecke to attack Eickhorst. Some time was lost by the Prince of Anhalt in driving the French out of Hahlen, and this caused a delay in the deployment of General von Spoerken's division. This deployment was covered by the guns of Captain Foy's battery of British artillery, which was joined soon by Captain Macbean's battery, and a Hanoverian brigade of heavy guns.

The French line of battle was semi-circular, conforming to the contour of the walls of Minden. The division of Broglie was on the right, near the Weser. The infantry was in the first line, and the cavalry in the second line, with two batteries in advance of the whole. On the left was half of the infantry and the main army, with thirty-four guns. In the centre of the heath were fifty-five squadrons of cavalry, and on the left of the cavalry was the remainder of the Infantry, with thirty guns.

The allied army was ready for action at seven o'clock. Its right was at the enclosures between the villages of Hartum and Hahlen, and its left was touching Stemmer. On the right was the infantry of General von Spoerken's division, and on the right of this division were the two British infantry brigades. When the British infantry formed, there was a fir-wood upon their right, in front of the 12th Regiment, through which some platoons of that regiment, and the 20th Regiment, which covered it in the second line, passed. This wood has now disappeared, and the land is under cultivation. The brigade of Brigadier-General Waldegrave formed the first line: from right to left, the regiments were the 12th, the 37th, and the 23rd. The brigade of Brigadier-General Kingsley formed the second line: from right to left, the regiments were the 20th, the 51st, and the 25th, and, beyond, were the Hanoverian battalions of Hardenberg, and two battalions of Hanoverian Guards. The brigade of Kingsley overlapped the leading brigade on both flanks.

Ferdinand who had watched the deployment sent an order that when the proper time had arrived, they were to advance with "drums beating". Through some mistake in the conveying of the order, or

The 25th Foot at Minden

through some misunderstanding of it, Waldegrave's brigade did not wait a moment, but at once marched off briskly, "drums beating". *Aides-de-camp* galloped to stop them. The brigade halted behind the fir-wood, where they remained for a few minutes while the second brigade was deploying. Before, however, the deployment was completed, the drums beat again a "rally", and off they went, followed by the second line, which had lost some distance in the deployment. In the first 150 yards, they were rent by a cross-fire from 60 guns: but, this did not stop, or even retard, them. They marched off, not to receive, but to attack cavalry. They suffered heavily, but they did not waver, and they maintained a magnificent bearing. And now, the French cavalry were set in motion, and eleven squadrons poured down upon them. They stood firm until the horsemen were within ten yards' distance, and then they poured in such a deadly volley, that the ground was covered with men and horses, and the remainder of the cavalry were scattered by the continued advances of the British and the Hanoverian infantry.

It was at this moment that Prince Ferdinand, seeing the effect of the infantry-fire, sent an order to Lord George Sackville to bring up the cavalry of the right, and to complete the destruction of the French. Sackville at first disputed the order, and then moved forward for a short distance, and halted. A second order was sent. The cavalry remained stationary. The Saxon infantry in four brigades with thirty-two guns came forward from the left of the French cavalry, to enfilade the British brigades. Ferdinand seeing this, and unable to move Sackville with his cavalry, ordered Phillips's brigade of heavy guns to advance and ward off the attack. Meanwhile, the French cavalry had rallied, and their second line charged the allies.

Under this three-fold attack of cavalry, artillery, and infantry, the British and Hanoverian troops wavered momentarily, but, closing their ranks, they gave the second line of cavalry a volley which sent them off the field in confusion. Then they attacked the Saxon infantry, shattering and hurling them back. To save the British regiments from annihilation, Ferdinand sent once more an *aide-de-camp* to Sackville, telling him to bring up the "British cavalry", imagining that there might be some latent thought of jealousy of the foreign cavalry in the mind of this officer. The message was delivered: but, not a squadron moved. Ferdinand reinforced the brigades, when a third attack on the nine battalions was made by a fresh body of French cavalry, which broke through the first line, and then, destroyed by the second, was

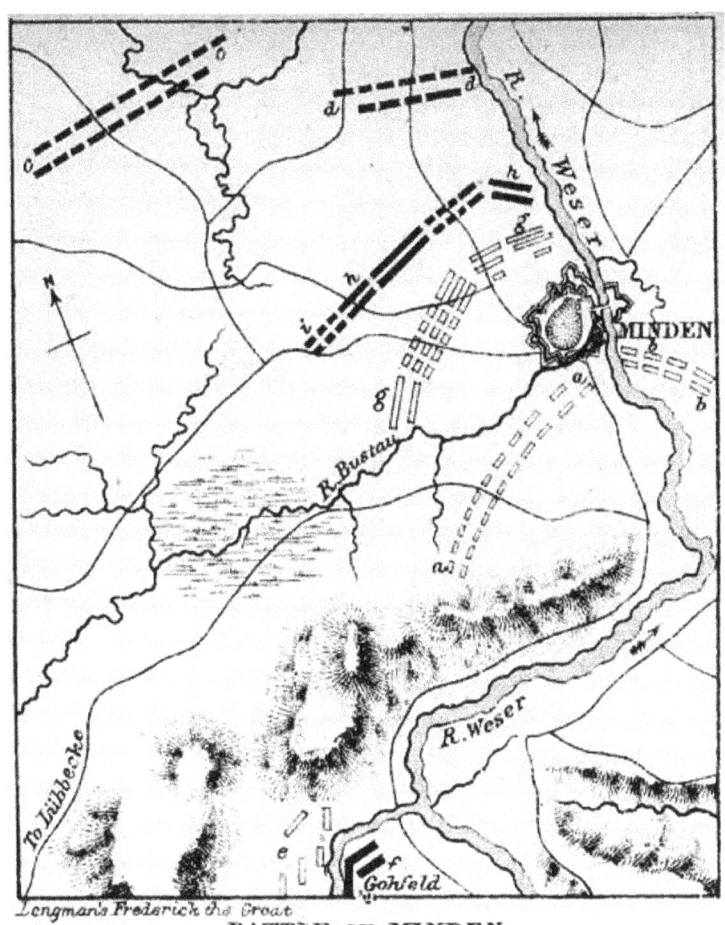

BATTLE OF MINDEN
August 1. 1759.

*a a*, French Army behind Minden, July 31.
*b b*, Broglio's detachment.
*c c*, The Allied Army, July 31.
*d d*, Wangenheim.
*e*, The Duc de Brissac.
*f*, The Hereditary Prince.
*g g*, French Army in battle order, August 1.
*h h*, Allied Army about to attack, August 1.
*i*, Cavalry under Sackville.

sent flying to the rear.

Ferdinand sent a fourth message to Sackville, which again met with no response. He sent then a *fifth aide-de-camp*, to bring up Lord Granby with the second line of cavalry; but, Sackville rode up, and ordered Granby not to move. Sackville now, with an astounding insolence, rode up to Ferdinand, and asked what the various orders might mean. "My Lord", Ferdinand replied, "the opportunity is now passed".

A complete junction had been made between Ferdinand and Wangenheim, and the gap of three miles had been filled. The guns of the Allies silenced those of the French. Ferdinand's left wing and the German Cavalry completed the defeat, and the French retreated under the guns of Minden to their positions behind the marsh. At ten o'clock the fight was over, and the chief honours of the battle were won by the six British and the three Hanoverian battalions, and by the British artillery. The corps of General von Wangenheim maintained pretty nearly the same position during the whole action.

The pursuit of the flying French was made by the British batteries of Captains Foy and Macbean moving rapidly along the border of the marsh, halting occasionally to fire upon the enemy, until they came opposite the bridges of the Bastau, where they unlimbered and kept up such a tempest of fire as demoralised the enemy, which fled in wild confusion.

The losses of the Allies in killed and wounded were 2,600 men, of this number 81 officers and 1,311 men were of the six British regiments: in other words, thirty *per cent*, of the British were killed and wounded, while the three Hanoverian battalions, which were on the left flank, lost twelve *per cent*. The two regiments which suffered the most were the twelfth, which lost 302, and the twentieth, which lost 326, of all ranks: they were in the post of honour on the right flank of their respective brigades.

The French in casualties, variously reported, lost from seven to eleven thousand. Further, they lost most of their baggage, seventeen standards, and forty-three guns. Afterwards, in their history of the battle, they said that all would have gone well, and that victory was already in their grasp, had it not been for the Manteaux (mantle, or cloak) corps of the Hanoverians, which fell upon them, and wrested victory from them. They had mistaken for the name of the battalion the cries "*Man tau, man tau!*" or, instead of dialect, "*Man zu, man zu!*", and "*Man tau, man drup!*", or, instead of dialect, "*Man zu, man darauf!*": "Up men! and, at them!".

Battle of Minden

The chief feature of the Battle of Minden was the attack of the British infantry, which, although it disorganised his plans, showed the generalship of Ferdinand, who supported them when they had advanced beyond recall. As a feat of gallantry, it has seldom if ever been surpassed. Marshal Contades said:

> I never thought to see a single line of infantry break through three lines of cavalry ranked in order of battle, and tumble them to ruin.

An officer who served in the British forces at Minden, referring to the six regiments of Infantry, stated that, notwithstanding the loss they sustained before they could get up to the enemy, notwithstanding the repeated attacks of the enemy's cavalry, notwithstanding a fire of musketry well kept-up by the enemy's infantry, notwithstanding their being exposed in front and flank, such was the unshaken firmness of those troops that nothing could stop them; and, the whole body of the French cavalry was totally routed.

The chief of Ferdinand's staff wrote:

> Never were so many boots and saddles seen on a battlefield, as opposite to the English and the Hanoverian Guards.

The artillery was directed by the Count Lippe-Bückeburg, The chief of the staff recorded that everyone did well, but that the British batteries did wonders. Captains Foy and Macbean, Drummond and Phillips, gained for themselves, and for the Royal Regiment of Artillery, immense fame.

The bravery at the Battle of Minden was not one-sided. A corps of French grenadiers, of which the commander's name was Perer, was exposed to a battery that carried off files at once. Not wishing them to fall back, this officer rode slowly down the front of the line with his snuff-box in his hand and, taking no notice of the bullets, said, "Well, my boys, what's the matter? Eh, cannon? Well, it kills you, it kills you, that's all, my boys; march on, and never mind it!"

Prince Ferdinand was a commander of ability, resource, and personality, and his appreciation of the Battle of Minden was conveyed to the Allied Army in a general order, of which the following is a translation:—

Südhemmern, August 2nd, 1759.

His Serene Highness commands the Adjutant-General von Reden, to express to the whole Army his best thanks for the great bravery which they showed yesterday, and especially for the good bearing, particularly of the British infantry, the two battalions of Hanoverian Guards, the whole of the cavalry of the left wing, and of the corps of Lieutenant-General von Wangenheim, and, in particular, the Dragoon Regiment of Holstein and the Hessian Cavalry, the *Regiment du Corps* and the Hammerstein Regiment of Hanover, and, not least, of the whole of the brigades of artillery. His Serene Highness hereby publicly declares that, next to God, he ascribes the victory of this day to the intrepidity and exceptionally good behaviour of these troops.

He assures them that his gratitude for it, as long as he lives, will never cease, and, in any way he can serve his brave troops, or any individual of them, it would be to His Excellency a great pleasure, should an opportunity arise. His Serene Highness commands the Adjutant-General von Reden to express in a very special manner his high esteem and gratitude to His Excellency General von Spoerken, to His Highness the Duke of Holstein, and to the Generals von Imhoff and Urff. His Serene Highness is infinitely obliged to His Excellency Count von Bückeburg for all the trouble and care which he took in every way, so that the Artillery were served yesterday with exceptional effect. Count von Reden is also commanded to express profuse gratitude to the commanding-officers of the brigades of artillery.

Colonel Brown, Lieutenant-Colonel von Huth, and Major Storken, and to the English Captains Phillips, Drummond and Foy. His Serene Highness is infinitely obliged to Majors-General Waldegrave and Kingsley for the extreme bravery with which they led forward their brigades.

His Serene Highness commands the following message to be conveyed to the Marquis of Granby, that he is convinced that had he been fortunate enough to have had him at the head of the cavalry of the right wing, his presence would have greatly assisted in bringing the day to a far more complete and more brilliant issue.

In conclusion. His Serene Highness commands that it may be made known to those who were immediately in touch with him, whose behaviour he especially admired, namely, the Duke of Richmond, Colonel Fitzroy, Captain Ligonier, Colonel Watson, Captain Wilson *aide-de-camp* to Major-General Waldegrave, Adjutant-General von Estorff, the Adjutants-in-Chief von Bülow, Derenthal, Count Taube and Malortie, that he has great reason for satisfaction with their bearing. Lastly, His Serene Highness desires and orders the generals of the army to carry out instantly and exactly, whatever the occasion maybe, any orders brought to them by his adjutants-in-chief.

Captain Macbean's name was inadvertently omitted, but this omission was made good by a special letter from Prince Ferdinand.

The six British regiments of infantry by their extraordinary bravery stand as an example of the highest ideal of combined courage and determination in the stress of battle. They took the initiative, and, although by an error they changed the plans of the general, they carried it through, with overwhelming powers of destruction hurled against them, to a triumphant victory. Their attack on the French cavalry showed the highest state of military discipline, coolness and courage.

Madame de Pompadour, in a letter to the wife of Marshal Contades, dated August, 1759, wrote:

> This horrible defeat at Minden is the most melancholy check that we have received during the whole war: I am sorry, both for your sake and for mine, that it should have been Monsieur de Contades who was there.

Ferdinand bestowed unstinted praise upon all his troops, except on the cavalry of the right under Lord George Sackville, in connection with which, in contrast to the brilliant performance of the infantry, we have the dark episode showing deliberate and persistent misbehaviour and disobedience on the part of a general. It is difficult to conceive that a general-officer, commanding a large force of cavalry, could stand by and watch six regiments of his own nation, one of which he had commanded, attacked by cavalry, artillery, and infantry, and not move to their assistance. It is incomprehensible that Lord George Sackville should have remained obdurate, and that he should have ignored five distinct orders to charge the enemy, and that then he should have prevented Lord Granby, his second in command, from acting.

Sackville had fought, and had been wounded, at Fontenoy. In private life, he had fought duels, which were presumably a test of courage; yet, Horace Walpole has recorded that the troops who were engaged under him at St. Malo openly asserted that he had no desire to meet the enemy. It is more than probable that at Minden he was influenced

Battle of Minden

by personal jealousy, or dislike, of Ferdinand. Lord George was the first Viscount Sackville. There is no doubt as to his ability, and he was, at one time, credited with the authorship of the *Junius Letters*, written between 1769 and 1772, severely inveighing against the conduct of the king, and of certain members of the government. He felt his self-sufficiency as a prominent member of one of the governing families, who, if not above receiving orders, was strong enough to be a law unto himself in circumstances in which he should have rendered obedience.

Sackville was commanded by George the Second to return to England, and in April, 1760, he was tried by court martial, found guilty of disobedience of orders, and adjudged unfit to serve His Majesty in any military capacity whatever. This sentence the king declared to be worse than death. George the Second died in October, and one of the- first recorded acts in the new reign is, that the court of George the Third "gave a cordial welcome to Lord George Sackville", and this, be it remembered, in the year following the Battle of Minden. A sufficient and just commentary upon this desecration of the kingly authority, is the reproach of posterity for the loss of the American Colonies, shared by George the Third and his Minister of War, Lord George Germain, otherwise Sackville.

WILLIAM PITT, EARL OF CHATHAM

CHAPTER 5

# Minden, and After

The year 1759 had come to an end. It was the worst year for Frederick, but for George the Second and England it was a year of great and momentous events. Pitt was the prime minister. On August 1st, there was the victory of Minden, and in six weeks to a day from that date was the capture by Wolfe of Quebec, and with it the conquest of Canada.

Wolfe fell mortally wounded. The loss of blood excites thirst, and the dying hero called for water.

"They run! they run!" exclaimed an officer near him.

"Who run?" cried Wolfe.

"The enemy", was the reply.

Then said he, "God be praised, I die happy."

This was on September 13th. Montcalm, his gallant French opponent, died the next day, and Quebec capitulated on September 18th, 1759. Had it not been for the employment of the large French force at Minden, Montcalm might have outmatched Wolfe by vastly greater strength.

On November 20th, Sir Edward Hawke destroyed the French Fleet in Quiberon Bay, with the result that France disappeared as a maritime power. The capture of the Island of Guadeloupe in the West Indies, and of the Island of Goree on the West Coast of Africa, followed by the withdrawal of the French Fleet from the East Indian Seas, completed for England a series of victories that are without parallel.

This year as Pitt designed it, and as the nation, and the people of his day, received and accepted it, was in reality the first year of the British Empire. Soldiers and sailors found, employed, and promoted, responded with a rare devotion to the genius of the Statesman by whom they were selected. Wolfe, the two Howes, Amherst, Anson, Hawke, and

Saunders won lasting fame. Wolfe was the first and greatest exponent of the power of a combination of sea and land forces. "Canada was won in Germany" was the expression of Pitt, and this famous expression was accepted as serious by Thomas Carlyle, John Richard Green, and Frederic Harrison: in fact, Carlyle and Green asserted that Pitt founded the United States of America.

Admiral Mahan attributes the success of England to her overwhelming power at sea. Julian S. Corbett, in his brilliant review of Naval Strategy in *England in the Seven Years' War*, says that to accept the above famous dictum is to misconceive Pitt's policy, and that he used it when he had won all that for which he wished, and when he was protesting against the government of King George the Third for their desertion of England's ally, Frederick the Great. The military historian J. W. Fortescue takes the larger view, that Pitt spoke half the truth, and that, in effect, not only Canada, and America, but also the East and the West Indies, in other words, the British Empire was won in Germany. This is the general verdict of posterity, a verdict which is not lessened by the difference of opinion amongst students and experts, as to the precise policy and means by which it was obtained.

CHAPTER 6

# The Campaign of 1760: Warburg

It was not until the middle of January, 1760, that the Allies were allowed to retire to their winter-quarters. Osnabrück (or, Osnaburg) was assigned to the British, and in that district, they remained until May 12th, when they were concentrated at Paderborn under the command of the Marquis of Granby. A week later Prince Ferdinand was with the main portion of the army at Fritzlar, while the British and the Prussians held the line from Coesfeld to Hamm. The Allies held these positions, the French remaining inactive until June 22nd, when Broglie advanced with one wing of the army from Giessen.

Ferdinand wished to force Broglie into action before he could effect a junction with the corps commanded by Count St. Germain. His design, however, was frustrated by an error of judgment on the part of General Imhoff, who withdrew the advanced corps to Kirchhain.

Broglie continued his advance, and, by the end of June, the two Armies were standing face to face in the neighbourhood of Neustadt, where they remained until July 8th, when Ferdinand learned that Broglie was moving with the evident intention of joining hands with St. Germain.

Ferdinand having ordered the whole army to advance, pushed forward the hereditary prince with a division, to seize the Heights of Corbach, commanding a defile through which the French must pass. The French, however, had the advantage of a good start, and those from the North under St. Germain had cleared the defile, and were forming in order of battle, when the hereditary prince reached the Plain of Sachsenhausen. It is supposed that Ferdinand saw only a portion of the enemy, or that he underestimated their numbers. However, this may have been, he decided at once to attack: but, the weight of numbers, and the continuous stream of reinforcements, inflicted upon him a heavy repulse, with a loss of 800 men and 19 guns. The hereditary prince covered the retreat of his main body, with the British infantry, and, when at one time the 5th, 24th, 50th, and 51st Regiments were seriously involved, he placed himself at the head of Bland's and Howard's (1st and 3rd) Dragoons, and made a gallant charge to save the infantry.

Such was the opening of the campaign for the year, and, for the Allies, it was a discouraging one: but, in spite of this and the fact that the French troops opposed to them numbered two to one, such was the confidence of the army in their leader and of the commander in his men, that morale compensated fully for disparity in numbers.

Broglie now appeared to be threatening the right flank of the Allies, and Ferdinand, therefore, detached a division under the Hereditary Prince to attack the French force commanded by General de Glaubitz.

On the morning of July 16th, the hereditary prince made a reconnaissance from Treysa with his mounted troops, and found the enemy in an opening of the mountains, with their left touching a forest at the village of Emsdorf, and their right sheltered behind the village of Erksdorf, in which they had not placed a single man. They were resting without piquets, guards, or any other precautions customary for an army operating in an enemy's country.

As soon as the infantry came up, the hereditary prince led them and a portion of the cavalry through the forest, making a detour, and brought them on to the left flank of the enemy, which was completely taken by surprise; and, before they could properly form, the prince's infantry had shattered them with a volley. One body fell back upon another; but, before they could get into proper formation. General Luckner, responding to the sound of the firing, charged with his cavalry, to the complete discomfiture of the French, who took refuge in the forest. They were pursued to Langenheim, where the Prussian infantry took possession of the bridge over the River Ohm. By this time, Elliott's Light Dragoons (the 15th) had come up on the right, and cut the enemy off from the road leading to Amöneburg. The dragoons and some hussars were led by the hereditary prince through a wood on to a plain, where they again charged the enemy who were heading for Nieder-Kleyn.

The dragoons charged the French four times, and at last succeeded in separating from the main force a body of 500, which they surrounded, and compelled to surrender. The French account of the ac-

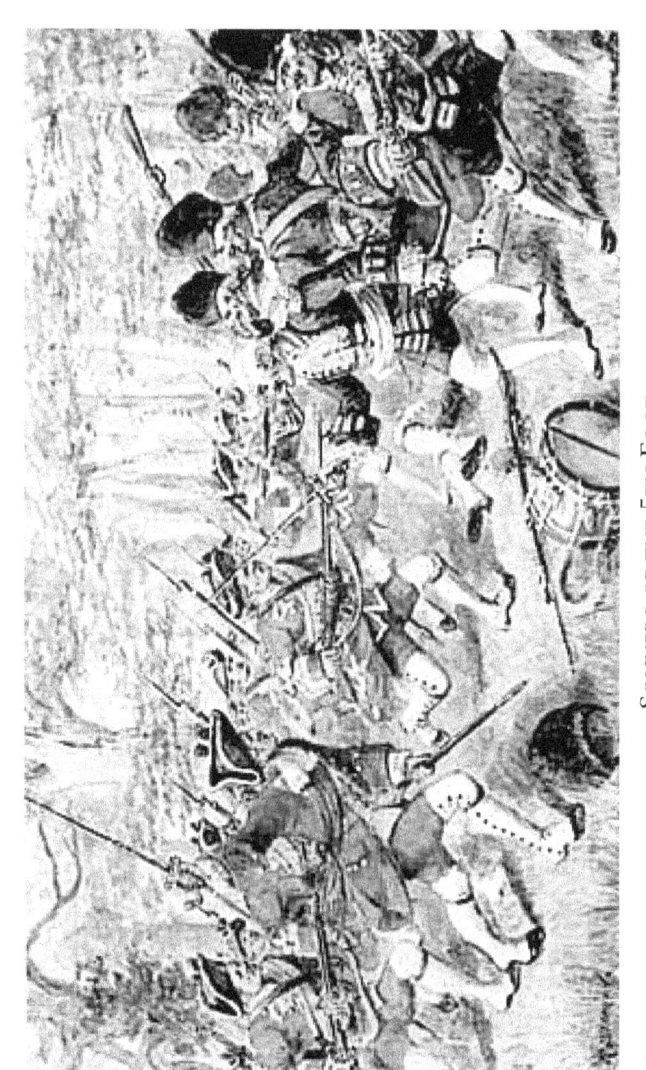

Soldiers of the 5th Foot

tion says, "the British cavalry gave them no respite".

Another body of the French which had occupied a wood near Nieder-Kleyn was attacked and surrendered. The French loss was heavy, the number of the prisoners alone being 2,500. The honours of the day fell to Elliott's Light Dragoons under Major Erskine: they charged the French four times, captured nine pairs of colours, and thus distinguished themselves in this their first engagement.

The subsequent movements of the French disclosed an intention of separating the division of General von Spoerken from the main body, and of cutting off the Allies from Cassel; and so, Ferdinand sent the hereditary prince to the general's assistance, while he with the main body made a night march to Cassel. Ferdinand's rear-guard was repeatedly pressed by the French during this march, and the march of the division of General von Spoerken was also much harassed, fighting constantly for two days in a most difficult country.

The object of Broglie was to cut the Allies off from Westphalia. Chevalier De Muy occupied Warburg, Broglie marched on lines parallel to Ferdinand, while a third body of the French kept a guard over Cassel.

Leaving General Kielmansegge to protect Cassel, Ferdinand decided to fall upon Muy at Warburg, and with this intention he crossed the Diemel between Liebenau and Dringleberg. Spoerken's division began the movement at 4 o'clock on the afternoon of July 29th. The division of the hereditary prince followed the same evening, and it included a British brigade, consisting of two battalions of grenadiers, two battalions of Highlanders, and four squadrons of cavalry. The main body left camp on the following night, crossed the Diemel at Liebenau in six columns, and on the morning of the 31st, it was arranged on the heights near Körbecke. The French had taken up a strong defensive position, their right resting on Warburg, and their left on the hill of Ossendorf. Fischer's corps held the town of Warburg.

Ferdinand resolved that the hereditary prince and General von Spoerken should turn the enemy's left flank at Ossendorf, while the main army under his direction made an attack in front. On the night of the 31st, the hereditary prince marched to Donkelburg in two columns, which he formed in two lines, with his left at Dössel, and his right near Grimbeke. Without loss of time, and perhaps with undue precipitation, he attacked the French and forced them to fall back upon Warburg. Ferdinand's men were marching at full speed to make the main assault on the front of the enemy's line, but they could not

7th Dragoons at Warburg

get up in time to second the flank attack of the hereditary prince. The march was so pressed that many men fell down in the ranks from over-exertion.

Ferdinand ordered the Marquis of Granby to bring the British cavalry into action as speedily as possible, and they covered the five miles at a sharp trot. As soon as the cavalry came within striking distance, Lord Granby deployed them into two lines, and led them personally against the French cavalry, of which the majority turned and fled. His hat fell off in the charge, and his uncovered bald head, shining in the sunlight, was a subject of good-natured merriment throughout the war. Turning aside from the pursuit of the enemy's cavalry, he launched his squadrons against their infantry, who left their ranks, throwing down their arms, and, crossing the River Diemel in wild disorder, took refuge in the town of Warburg.

The British artillery under Captain Phillips galloped to the bank of the Diemel, and kept up such an incessant fire, that the French were prevented from reforming on the opposite bank of the river. An attack was then made upon Warburg, when the enemy began a general retreat, and were pursued by the cavalry under Lord Granby. In this battle, the British cavalry, under another commander, redeemed the credit which they had lost at Minden. Of the infantry, the British grenadiers—that is to say, the grenadier companies from all the regiments, fighting as two grenadier battalions—according to authentic accounts, performed wonders. Colonel Beckwith, who commanded the brigade, was wounded. The French lost 1500 men killed and wounded, two thousand prisoners, and ten guns. The British lost 590 men killed and wounded, and, of these, 415 were grenadiers and Highlanders.

It may be added that Colonel Beckwith was one of Wolfe's captains. He distinguished himself as a brigadier throughout the Seven Years' War. At the close of the war, he left the English service, and became the second-in-command of the Free-Corps of 6,000 men, formed by Frederick. Finding that his finances would not admit of his retaining it, he disbanded the corps, refusing claims for compensation with the remark, "you get nothing, you stole like ravens".

After the fight at Warburg, there was a pause until August 22nd, when the hereditary prince crossed the Diemel at the head of 1,200 men, to harass the left flank of the enemy, which took refuge in the town of Zierenberg. He determined now to attempt a surprise. On September 5th, he ordered five battalions, a detachment of Highland-

BATTLE OF WARBURG

ers, and eight squadrons of cavalry, to be ready to leave their camp at 8 o'clock in the evening. Tents were to remain standing. The column was led by Maxwell's grenadiers, a detachment of Kingsley's, and the Highlanders. After marching about three miles from the Diemel, they were met by the Light Troops, who were to assist in the attack by intercepting any of the enemy attempting to enter, or to leave, Zierenberg.

The Greys and the Inniskillings were in position at a wood near Malzberg, and Malzberg was held by a battalion of grenadiers. Two infantry regiments and some dragoons were posted at intervals between Malzberg and Zierenberg to cover the retreat, if necessary. On reaching a mill about two miles from the town of Zierenberg, and in sight of the enemy's main guard. Maxwell's grenadiers, Kingsley's regiment, and the Highlanders separated, each taking a different road to the town. They were challenged by the piquets, who made no attempt to reconnoitre. The three bodies advanced in silence: but, in pushing their way through some gardens, the noise of their trampling feet was heard, and this gave the alarm to the enemy, who began to fire.

The grenadiers, with firelocks unloaded, rushed through the piquets, disposed of the guard at the gate, and entered the town. The surprise was so complete, that the French could not gather together in any strong formation, but took to the houses, from which they fired upon the British in the streets. The houses were cleared at the point of the bayonet, the loss of the enemy exceeding one hundred men, while the attacking party had only ten casualties, which was considered wonderful in a night-attack. The account by the French general expresses great admiration for the silence and intrepidity of Colonel Beckwith's grenadiers in making the attack. The prince ordered a retreat at 3 o'clock, and the camp at Warburg was reached at 6 o'clock on the morning of the 6th.

Wesel, the base for one-half of Broglie's army was an alluring object for Prince Ferdinand. If he could seize it the French would be cut adrift. Three weeks were spent in making preparations for a siege. Towards the end of September everything was ready, and a heavy siege-train of artillery under Count Lippe-Bückeburg, with an escort of 10,000 men, under the command of the hereditary prince, marched for Wesel. Broglie, on hearing of this movement, despatched a strong corps under the Marquis de Castries to follow them. To counteract this, Ferdinand sent ten battalions of British infantry and three regiments of cavalry to reinforce the hereditary prince.

Charge of the 6th Inniskillings at Warburg

The French general was strengthened still further, and the hereditary prince decided to bring matters to a conclusion. The French were in number superior to the Allies, and they held a very strong position. In their front was a canal. Their right rested on Rheinberg, and their left was covered by the convent known as Kloster Kampen and the village of Kampenbroecke. Access to Kampenbroecke was possible only through a wooded morass, and communication between the village and the convent was by a bridge over the canal. To reach the French camp, it was necessary to pass the bridge and the convent, and both were held by Fischer's irregular corps of 7,000 men. By surprise alone could the hereditary prince effect his purpose.

On October 15th, at ten o'clock at night, the force marched from their camp, and early on the morning of the 16th, the leading division came upon the French outposts, about half a league from Kloster Kampen. Contrary to orders some shots were fired, and the bridge was seized. The French irregulars, separated from their main body, were attacked and overwhelmed. The firing had now alarmed the French camp.

Meanwhile, the hereditary prince at the head of the British grenadiers made his way into the village of Kampenbroecke, which fell into his hands before the French were aware of his presence. A French officer, visiting his outposts, came upon the prince, and at the cost of his life gave the alarm. Battalions were hurried into the fight, which now became general in the village and in the adjoining wood. Although outnumbered, the prince continued the struggle, the British and the Hanoverians fighting with great gallantry, until he was wounded and the ammunition had failed, when they gave way.

If the British reserves under General Howard had come up when they were sent for, they would have saved the day: but, their failure was the result of a pure misadventure. They arrived, however, in time to cover the retreat, though the French pursuit had been checked previously by a very gallant charge of Elliott's Light Dragoons (15th). This was a very stubborn and sanguinary battle, "a many-winged intricate night-battle," according to Carlyle. The French lost 2,630 men killed and wounded, and between three and four hundred prisoners. The Allies lost 1,300 men killed and wounded, a considerable number of prisoners, two guns, and one pair of colours.

The siege of Wesel was raised, and earlier than usual, on account of the inclemency of the weather and the impassable condition of the roads, Ferdinand ordered the army into winter quarters, the British being assigned to the line of the Diemel and Wesel.

In a letter to the Marquis de Castries, dated November, 1760, Madame de Pompadour writes:

> I thank you for your letter, and especially for your victory (at Kloster Kampen). This little affair with the Prince of Brunswick is a consolation in the torrent of calamities which pours upon us from all sides. . . . The Prince of Brunswick is always to be feared, and his retreat is not that of a man who is afraid.

CHAPTER 7

# Vellinghausen: 1761

The new year, 1761, was opened by the French with a surprise-attack on the post of Stadtberg, commanded by Major de Laune, a valiant soldier, who died fighting rather than allow himself to fall into their hands. No less than 180 men were made prisoners in this affair.

De Laune was a friend of Wolfe, who described him as being formed by nature for service in an American Campaign. He served with the rifle-men commanded by the Honourable William Howe, who led the advance up the Heights of Abraham: they were both trained by Wolfe, and de Laune was a beneficiary under his will to the extent of £100. Major de Laune is the hero of a work of fiction entitled *Amyott Brough*. Representatives of his family live, (as at 1914), at Sharsted Court, Sittingbourne,

Several untoward incidents followed, and among them was the failure of two or three combinations projected for the conquest of Hesse. Ferdinand was obliged to retire from the Ohm to the Eder, as Broglie was making a rapid advance in overwhelming strength.

The hereditary prince at Gruenberg was attacked by three divisions of Cavalry. The column at his right flank was concealed by a wood: and, as the Hanoverian troops were entering a defile they were attacked, and 2,000 of them were made prisoners. This unfortunate loss allowed Ferdinand no option but to raise the siege of Cassel, which occurred on the last day of March, and once more the Army was sent into winter-quarters for a long and much-needed rest.

The French Court, tired and worn out by the drain upon their army and their financial resources, decided to make in the campaign this year a supreme effort to bring the war to a close; and so, they raised the army commanded by Prince Soubise, called the Army of the Rhine, to 100,000 men, and the army under Broglie, to 60,000 men. Their plan of campaign was as follows. Soubise was to attack Ferdinand and draw his attention, while Broglie advanced into Hanover. Ferdinand had only 100,000 men to meet 160,000 men of the enemy.

On March 27th, the Allies crossed the Eder, the passage being covered by the hereditary prince. The French remained dormant from this date to the end of June, when Soubise crossed the Rhine and advanced to Dortmund. Ferdinand concentrated his army at Paderborn. On the 19th, the Allies, with the exception of General von Spoerken's Corps, were encamped on the heights of Neuhaus, and two days later they marched in six columns to Geseke. Early in July, Ferdinand by a forced march brought his army in rear of that of Soubise at Dortmund. When the latter moved to Soest, Ferdinand followed him.

By July 10th, the French were nearly twice the strength of the Allies, who were at Hohenover. Between July 10th and 15th, the French marshals had made frequent reconnaissances of Ferdinand's position which extended along a range of heights from the River Lippe, on which his left flank rested, to Hilbeck.

The hereditary prince commanded the corps on the right of the line, from the village of Hilbeck, which he covered in the form of a crescent, to Illingen. This village stood between the left of the hereditary prince and the right of General Conway's corps, consisting of the brigade of guards and the infantry brigades of Townshend and Douglas. Conway's corps formed almost an echelon with the stream known as Salz Bach in their front. The River Aasse on their left, which could be crossed only by a bridge, separated them from Howard's corps, composed of the brigades of Lord Pembroke and of Lord Frederick Cavendish, which stood in front of the hamlet of Kirch Dinker.

On the left of Howard, and between him and Lord Granby, the line was continued by the corps commanded by the Prince of Anhalt. The British brigades of Beckwith, Sandford and Harvey, under Lord Granby, held the salient point of Ferdinand's line, and they were on the heights above Vellinghausen, which was in their front. The extreme left of the position on the River Lippe was defended by the corps of Generals Wutgenau and Wolfe. The Salz Bach was an almost impassable quagmire, except at the village of Scheidingen, which was about three-quarters of a mile in advance of Illingen. These two villages marked the centre of the allied line of defence.

The French plan was to concentrate their main attack on Granby's position, while Soubise was to draw the attention of Ferdinand by assailing Scheidingen, and to embarrass him further by sending a col-

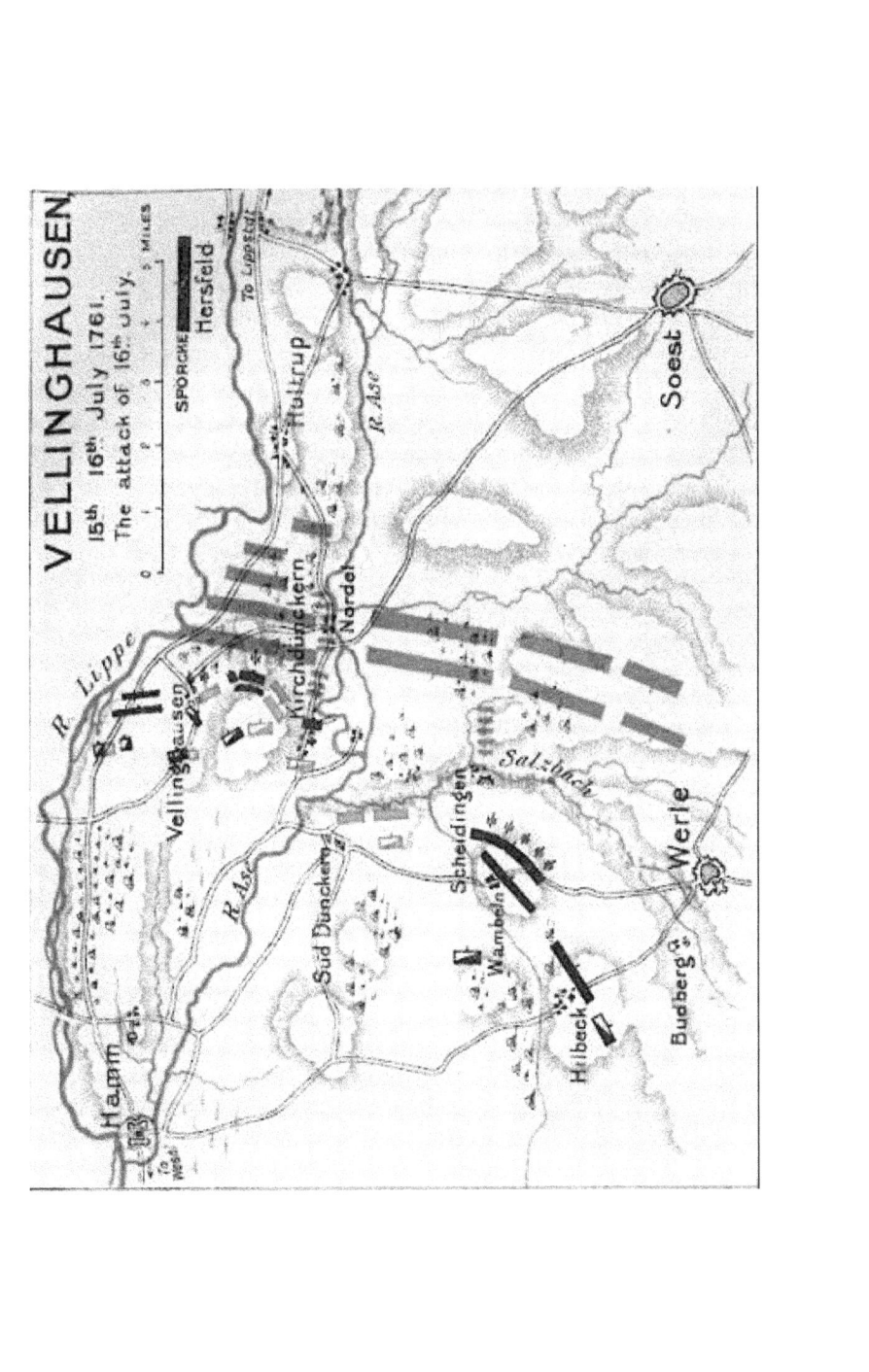

umn to work round the right of the hereditary prince. On the evening of July 15th, the French drove in Granby's outposts from Haus Nehele and occupied the village of Nordel (or, Narteln). Through some mistake, Wutgenau's corps was not in the position assigned to it, and it was surprised in its camp. Granby's troops also were surprised, but quickly got into position, and held their ground until Wutgenau's troops came into fighting line. The French continued the attack until 10 o'clock, and, even if their effort was premature, they gained some advantages.

As it was obvious that Broglie, who commanded the French right, intended to carry Granby's position, Ferdinand strengthened that part of his line during the night of the 15th, and massed his artillery on Granby's left front. These tactical movements caused unrest and some small combats during the hours between dark and dawn. At 3 o'clock on the morning of the 16th, the French marshal resumed the fight by attacking Wutgenau, and at the same time the French artillery tried to secure the hill which commanded Granby's position. Ferdinand ordered the British battalions of Majors Maxwell, Campbell and Keith, with some Hanoverian battalions, to seize this height. This they accomplished with great resolution and intrepidity, Maxwell's battalion making prisoners of the regiment of Rouge, consisting of four battalions, with its guns and colours. The hereditary prince being harassed by a heavy artillery-fire, Ferdinand went to his assistance with Lord Frederick Cavendish's brigade: but, before they reached him, the French had desisted.

Three attacks on the passages of the Salz Bach in the centre of the allied position were made simultaneously, two being feints, while the real attack was delivered against the bridge and village of Scheidingen, which were carried. Here they were checked by the defenders of an old redoubt, who repulsed seven vigorous attacks. The Irish brigade made an effort to carry this part of the allied position, but they were driven back with considerable loss.

Broglie having failed to make any impression on the allied left, withdrew his force, and so came to an end the Battle of Vellinghausen. The French casualties were over 5,000 men, with the loss of nine guns and six colours. The Allies lost 300 men killed, and 1,000 men wounded.

Numerous small affairs of outposts, attacks of isolated positions, and harassing movements, followed Vellinghausen, but nothing calling for detailed description.

In November, the army went into cantonments near Eimbeck, and, early in December, into winter-quarters, the British being located in the Bishopric of Osnaburg.

CHAPTER 8

# Wilhelmsthal and Amöneburg: 1762

The campaign of 1762 opened with the knowledge common to all ranks, that the government of George the Third was determined to bring about peace, and to withdraw British support from Frederick. This knowledge naturally produced a feeling of disquietude, and no doubt, unconsciously, it induced a spirit of carelessness and indifference to many of the minor details and precautions necessary on active service. The government did not fill up the depleted ranks of the regiments, and this delayed the commencement of active operations by Ferdinand. However, in spite of these drawbacks, this able commander was first in the field. On May 24th, he made a reconnaissance of the French position near Göttingen.

The main army of the French was commanded now by Marshals Soubise and d'Estrees, who had 80,000 men under their immediate command. The second army, called the Army of the Rhine, was under the Prince of Condé.

The negotiations for peace on the part of the British Government had one advantage for Ferdinand, inasmuch as the French were induced to remain stationary, instead of acting upon the offensive. The line which they then held was roughly one from Cassel to Göttingen, Göttingen being about 60 miles south-east of Hanover. Ferdinand sent the hereditary prince to watch the army under Condé, while he prepared to attack Soubise. By June 20th, Granby and the British were at Warburg, the main body of the Allies being concentrated at Körbecke. General Luckner was posted to observe a French corps under Prince Xavier, encamped between Werra and Göttingen with, as it was anticipated, the intention of raiding Hanover. Luckner was ordered also to seize the castle of Zappaburg, so as to secure the woods with the roads through them, and keep open communications with

Ferdinand.

On June 22nd, the French marshals moved from Cassel to Grebenstein, their centre occupying a commanding eminence. The headquarters took possession of the castle of Wilhelmsthal. They took no precautions to secure their right flank which rested on the forest Reinhard Wald, or to make safe the passes and ravines in their front. One corps under Castries was at Karlsdorf, perilously in advance of, and isolated from, the main army.

Ferdinand was not the general to let slip for a single day such a tempting opportunity, even though the enemy exceeded him in strength by 20,000 men. General Luckner, with six battalions of grenadiers, four squadrons of horse, and a regiment of hussars, was ordered to cross the Weser and make for Gottsbüren, about two miles north of Zappaburg. The Hessian Hussars near Mohringen screened this movement from Prince Xavier. Luckner marched from Hollenstadt at 6 o'clock on the morning of the 23rd, passed the Weser at Bodenfelde at 6 o'clock in the evening, and at 8 o'clock was at Gottsbüren.

The whole army was under arms at midnight. Ferdinand's dispositions were as follows:—He proposed to advance in the centre with five columns, consisting of twelve battalions of British Infantry, eleven battalions of Brunswickers, eight battalions of Hessians, the British cavalry, and part of the German cavalry. His route lay between Liebenau and Sielen, which he calculated would bring him to the front of the French position. The Marquis of Granby, who passed the Diemel at Warburg with two battalions of British grenadiers, two battalions of Highlanders, two British and two Hanoverian regiments of cavalry, and three regiments of Hanoverian infantry, with artillery, marched in two columns by parallel roads to Zierenberg, joining hands by 7 o'clock on the heights of Furstenwald, whence they were to strike the left flank of the French.

General von Spoerken's corps of twelve battalions of Hanoverians, and part of the cavalry of the left wing, marched between Hümme and Beverlec, so as to attack the right flank of Castries's division at Hombressen. Luckner was to move from Gottsbüren to Udenhausen, where he was to fall upon the rear of Castries. Colonel Reidesel, with sixteen squadrons of irregular cavalry, was to push forward from Zappaburg, and to extend Luckner's left. Each had his task accomplished punctually by 7 o'clock.

Spoerken with his corps reached the heights of Hombressen in the early morning, when, failing to discover the French, he took a wrong direction, which brought him in front of the enemy's position. This false move ruined the whole of Ferdinand's plans.

Castries in alarm hastily withdrew his cavalry, hiding the movement from Spoerken. The arrival of Luckner's corps at Udenhausen added to the confusion. Coming upon Spoerken's regiment, Luckner was fired upon by them, mistaking his division for the enemy, and, during this complication, Castries had time to extricate his corps. Moreover, the attack on the right of the French main body was delayed by Spoerken's men firing on those of Luckner.

The French, although surprised and in complete confusion, broke up their camp, and in a marvellously short time formed up on the heights; and, the obstinate adherence of General Kielmansegge to the letter of his instructions, although they were impracticable, saved the French from being cut off in their retreat.

The advance of the five columns under Ferdinand was retarded by the unlucky corps of Spoerken, which, being out of its place, caused a fatal delay.

Granby was true to the moment in his position, which, on its discovery, was an alarming one for the French, who discerned how skilfully the web had been drawn around them. To cover the retreat of the main body was now an object of vital importance to the French commanders.

General de Stainville occupied the wood of Meijenbreckfen, a hamlet near Wilhelmsthal, with the grenadiers of France, the Royal Grenadiers, the regiment of Aquitain, and some other troops, described in all contemporary accounts as "the flower of the French Army."

Granby's infantry consisted of three battalions of guards, the grenadiers, namely, the grenadier companies from all the regiments, in three battalions, and the 5th and the 8th Foot. As they approached the wood. General de Stainville attacked them, but Granby sent in more battalions, and drove the French back. It now became a hand to hand struggle. Granby was gradually surrounding the whole area of the wood, when Ferdinand's men came up and put an end to the stubborn conflict.

There were 1,500 Frenchmen killed or wounded, and 3,000 were taken prisoners by the 5th Foot. Only two battalions of the French escaped. The regimental grenadiers of Colonel Beckwith's brigade gained particular distinction in this fight. The 5th Foot won lasting fame by the capture of the three thousand prisoners, and, as a special honour, they were allowed to wear the caps of the French grenadiers. This is the origin of the wearing of fusilier caps, or busbies, in the British Army.

The Allies lost 700 men, 450 of them belonging to Granby's division. Had it not been for the error of judgment on the part of General von Spoerken, and the failure of Kielmansegge, the French Army would have been surrounded, surprised, and destroyed.

The French withdrew to the other side of the Fulda, and encamped at Landwerhagen, while Ferdinand occupied the heights between Holtzhausen and Weimer. The commander on either side was watching for some movement that would provide a favourable opportunity, but each was too cautious.

Before August 1st, the rival armies were on opposite banks of the River Fulda. On the 16th, the French evacuated the town of Göttingen, having destroyed the ramparts, magazines, etc., and moved to Vilbel, north of Frankfurt. The Allies followed on parallel lines. Condé, though closely pursued by the hereditary prince who wished to prevent a junction, joined Soubise on August 30th, and, on the same day, an attack was made by the hereditary prince, who suffered a severe repulse from the combined forces of the enemy.

There was now a race between the two armies, Ferdinand appreciating the design of the French marshals to cut him off from Cassel, which it had been his intention to besiege. Accordingly, he headed the advance-guard of the enemy at Wetter, and, on September 15th, he offered battle to Soubise. The French marshal, however, was not for fighting; but, on the contrary, he retreated at once, repassed the Lahn, and took up a position along the line of the Ohm. Ferdinand forced him again to the opposite side of the river.

The extreme left of his position was at the town of Amöneburg, which stands in the valley of the Ohm on the western, or left bank, of the river, and, as the French narrative describes it, "in the middle of the king's army." A stone bridge crossed the river near the castle of Amöneburg, Close to the bridge, and on the right side of the river near Ferdinand's position stood a mill, called the Bruecken-Muehle, with a courtyard and a cluster of houses. The bridge was commanded by a strong redoubt, and into this Ferdinand placed 200 men of Hardenberg's corps. In the town and castle of Amöneburg there were 500 men of the British Legion.

The French marshals resolved to capture the whole position. On August 19th, they made a reconnaissance, invested the castle on the night of the 20th, and, in the early morning of the 21st, made a sudden and unexpected attack on the castle, the bridge, and the redoubt. The walls of the castle were seriously damaged; but, it held out until the following evening. The most determined efforts were directed against the bridge and the mill, where the fighting was desperate, Hardenberg's men being most conspicuous.

Above and behind the mill was a hill upon which was encamped the corps of Zastrow. The French gradually increased their fighting line, and the intensity of their attacks, both by artillery and by musketry-fire. At 8 o'clock, after three hours' fighting, without a moment's respite, the fog cleared, and the strength of the dispositions of the attacking-force could be seen. General Zastrow came to the assistance of the defenders of the redoubt. He relieved the survivors of Hardenberg's force by 200 fresh men, sending them down the side of the hill in batches of fifty, on a widely-scattered front. Meanwhile, he ranged all his guns on the hill, to beat down if possible the fire of the French cannon, which numbered by this time thirty pieces. By noon, nine of Zastrow's guns were silenced. Every hour the men in the redoubt were relieved.

Ferdinand was brought upon the scene by the heavy firing, and he decided to hold the bridge and the redoubt at all costs. He ordered Granby's corps to come up at once from Kirchhain, to reinforce Zastrow. At four o'clock, Granby with three battalions of guards, two battalions of Highlanders, and twelve German guns came into action. The French likewise brought up reinforcements. Assault after assault was made upon the bridge: more than thirty French guns were firing upon a narrow frontage not exceeding 400 paces.

Men were sent into the redoubt, as quickly as they could pass down the side of the hill, in single file. The breastwork of the redoubt was so badly damaged that the defenders were compelled to pile up the bodies of the slain, and from this rampart they kept the enemy at bay. At seven o'clock, the French made their final and supreme effort, rushing the bridge and reaching the redoubt, only to be driven back, or destroyed, by the defenders. At eight o'clock, as the light was failing, after a fight of fourteen hours without pause, or cessation, all was over, and the French withdrew repulsed and crushed.

This was the last battle of the Seven Years' War in which the British fought under Prince Ferdinand of Brunswick. The French acknowledged a loss of 1,100 killed and wounded, and 800 was the loss of the Allies.

In a letter to the Marshal de Soubise, dated 1762, Madame de Pompadour wrote:

> Who is this brave Luckner, of whom people talk to me, who has gained so much glory at our expense? One must admit that the English are served too well. Especially do I hate, while I recognize his value, the Marquis of Granby, who ought to share, at least to the extent of half, the glory of the Prince Ferdinand.

The last Battle of the Seven Years' War was fought at Freyberg on October 29th, 1762, when the Prussians under Prince Henry, brother of Frederick, defeated with heavy loss the combined army of the Austrians and the Reich.

According to Frederick, Prince Henry was the only general who made no mistake during the war.

CHAPTER 9

# Peace

The Seven Years' War with all its brilliant victories would not be complete, even in this story, without some reference to the withdrawal of England from it. The preliminaries were signed in November, 1762. These were regarded by Frederick the Great on the one hand, and by Pitt on the other, as the act of desertion of an Ally, and in direct opposition to the terms of the Convention of Westminster, which enjoined that neither power should enter into a separate treaty for peace.

Towards the end of the reign of George the Second, there arose in England a political faction which was hostile to the wishes and to the policy of the king.

The name "Leicester-House Party" was given to a number of prominent persons who frequented the residence of the Dowager Princess of Wales, the mother of George the Third, an intriguer who played off the different political groups of the day against each other. The princess was opposed to the king, and his son the Duke of Cumberland, and their feeling towards her was one of hatred. She was antagonistic to Henry Fox (the first Lord Holland), and the Duke of Newcastle, and she was suspected of having caused the rupture between Pitt and Fox. She dominated the Prince of Wales, and her influence over him was regarded as pernicious. When the Prince of Wales came of age, the king intimated that it was his desire that the heir-apparent should receive a yearly allowance of £40,000, with a suitable residence.

These proposals were made, and by them the king hoped to draw the prince away from his mother. He, however, accepted the allowance, and then begged to be permitted to live with her, asking, moreover, that the Earl of Bute, his mother's favourite, should be appointed Groom-of-the-Stole to himself. The grant of the allowance could not

George III

be rescinded, but the request regarding Bute was contested warmly both by the king and by the Cabinet. From the pen of his governor, we have a portrait of the prince when he succeeded his grandfather, George the Second. Waldegrave says:

> He was inherently honest, but lacking in frankness, indolent, and yet sullenly obstinate, and—partly from his narrow education—strongly prejudiced.

This is not a pleasing picture, but it bears out the facial description that, when angry or opposed, "he threw back his eyes and ears like a vicious horse."

George the Second died, at Kensington, on October 25th, 1760, and one of the first acts of the new sovereign, George the Third, the son of Frederick Prince of Wales and the grandson of George the Second, was to welcome to his Court Lord George Sackville, who in the previous April, for his conduct at Minden, had been disgraced by the sentence of a general court-martial, with the approval of the king, the nation, and the army. This was a bad beginning for the new reign, and one of its direct effects was the disastrous loss of the American Colonies, and the blame for that loss has to be justly apportioned between George the Third, Lord George Germain, formerly Lord George Sackville, and Lord North as prime minister.

In a letter, dated November 6th, 1760, Madame de Pompadour wrote:

> I do not know if the death of the old King George (the Second) will effect any change in our affairs. . . The new king (George the Third) is very young; he ought to hate Pitt as much as his grandfather (George the Second) hated him; but, this minister will retain his office in spite of him, because he is in favour with the people.

In the first speech from the throne of George the Third, the earliest public intimation was made that there would be a reversal of the brilliant foreign policy of Pitt, who, in the brief period of five years, had established the supremacy of England at sea, and founded the British Empire as we know it today.

Pitt recognised the crisis at hand. He foresaw that Spain intended to declare war against England, and he wished to anticipate this before the Spanish ships crossed the Atlantic: but, he was defeated in the Cabinet by Bute and "the king's friends," and he resigned. As soon as the Treasure Ships were safely in port, Spain declared war, and this was the first humiliation of George the Third.

The king and Bute were urgent in their desire for peace, and this they conveyed to Frederick early in 1762, and, in the following May, the subsidy, agreed to by the Convention of Westminster, was refused.

The proposals for peace were not popular, while the chief advocate, Bute, that "Buzzard of a minister" as Frederick called him, was detested. The nation was with Pitt, and the king was with Bute. Henry Fox, the rival of Pitt, was brought in to lead the House of Commons, so as to ensure speedy peace, the preliminaries of which were first notified by the king, who pledged beforehand the faith of the nation, and then submitted them to the House of Commons. Meanwhile Fox was at work upon individual, and groups of, members. He showed the skill of a practised manipulator. To some he held out the tempting baits of office, employment, and sinecures, to others bare-faced bribery. At the office of the paymaster-general, votes were bought and sold, and, in one morning alone, the sum of £25,000 was paid to members, to support the policy of the king and Bute.

The far-seeing statesmanship of Pitt was never clearer than in his opposition to the Clause giving France fishing-rights three leagues from the shore of Newfoundland, and in the Gulf of St. Lawrence. That unfortunate concession has been, since 1762 down to the present day, a constant source of contention and of trouble between England and France.

By the treaty, England secured all Canada, and restored to France the Islands of Guadeloupe, Marie-Galante, la Desirade, Martinique and St. Lucia, retaining St. Vincent, Tobago, Dominica, and Grenada. The Island of Goree was handed back to France, and also certain conquests in India. Minorca and Belle Isle were exchanged. Manilla, which had been taken by an English Squadron in September, was returned. Wesel, Glatz, Cleves and Gueldres were ceded to Frederick the Great, and he retained Silesia.

From the French point of view, Madame de Pompadour wrote:

> We are ready to yield willingly Canada to the English: much good may it do them! But, as to the Islands and Pondicherry, we must save them at all cost.

And, in another letter:

> In what times we are living, alas! Could I have ever believed that I should live long enough to see Louis "*le Bien-Aimé*" become

an object of pity, to whom an arrogant victor offers terms of peace, as a matter of grace? A soldier, who served in the last war under Marshal de Saxe, replied one day to some strangers who asked him to what country he belonged, 'I have the honour of being a Frenchman'. Who would dare to say as much today?

Such were the general terms of peace, hastily and carelessly concluded, which deprived England of much that was hers by the right of conquest. The nation did not like it, and, for the Government, it aroused the deep and lasting hatred of Frederick; and, it left England without a friend in Europe.

For the time being, there was peace: perpetual peace is but a dream. So, Frederick the Great, towards the end of his life, wrote to Voltaire:

> I am old, cheerful, gouty, good-humoured. . . For the future, I cannot vouch. Running over the pages of history, I see that ten years never pass without a war. This intermittent fever may have moments of respite, but cease, never!

CHAPTER 10

# General-Field-Marshal Ferdinand, Prince of Brunswick and Lüneburg

Ferdinand, Prince of Brunswick, was born at Wolfenbüttel on January 12th, 1721. He was the sixth child, and the fourth son, of the fourteen children of Prince Ferdinand Albert, who was for the brief space of six months the reigning Prince of Brunswick. He was carefully brought up, and well educated. His military training began in his boyhood, and in July, 1740, when he was only 19 years of age, he was appointed to the command of the 39th Infantry Regiment, a corps raised in Brunswick for service in the Prussian Army. In the raising of the new Regiment, the youthful commander gained invaluable experience in military routine and organisation.

During the invasion of Silesia, Ferdinand acted as *aide-de-camp* to Frederick the Great, and, in his first experience of warfare at the Battle of Mollwitz, in April, 1741, he proved his bravery and resourcefulness. These qualities marked his conduct at the Battle of Chotustitz in May of the following year. In this campaign, he earned what was difficult to attain, the commendation of the king, who, when peace was declared, conferred upon him the Order of the Black Eagle, and promoted him to the rank of major-general.

Ferdinand fought at the head of his regiment in the campaign of 1744. In the Battle of Hohenfriedberg, on June 4th, 1745, when Frederick defeated the Austrians, seventy thousand men being engaged on each side, Ferdinand commanded a brigade. Three months later, at the Battle of Söhr, he conspicuously distinguished himself, although wounded, in leading his brigade to attack a range of heights defended under the shelter of a copse, which concealed the strength of the position, and in storming successfully the heights and capturing five

Ferdinand Duke of Brunswick

guns. In this fight, it happened curiously, unusual in the history of war and of families, that one of the defenders of the Austrian position was Prince Ludwig, a younger brother of Ferdinand.

Of this action Frederick wrote, that Ferdinand had surpassed himself and had contributed largely to the victory, and, as a reward, he conferred upon him the reversion of an estate. When the king made his triumphal entry into Berlin in the following December, Ferdinand had the place of honour by his side. In the Spring of 1750, the king was so pleased with the ability he displayed at the manoeuvres, that he promoted him lieutenant-general, and five years later he was appointed Governor of Magdeburg.

The Seven Years' War brought Ferdinand again into the field. He commanded the right of the three columns, in which formation Frederick crossed the border into Saxony and surrounded the Saxon Army at Parna, and, on September 13th, 1756, he commanded the Prussian vanguard that drove the Saxons out of Nollendorf. At the Battle of Lobositz, on October 1st, 1756, he commanded the Infantry of the Prussian right wing.

The winter of 1756-57 Ferdinand spent with Frederick at Dresden, where he had the advantage of preparing for the coming campaign and of discussing all the business of State with the "Great Master".

The confidence of Frederick at the opening of the campaign of 1757 was supreme, and a general of less eminence could not have had the temerity to write:

> We will see this Spring what Prussia is and that by our force, especially by our discipline, we will come to the end of the number of the Austrians, and of all those who oppose us.

Ferdinand captured Assig, on April 23rd, which was a good omen for a successful year's campaign, and, at the Battle of Prague, on May 6th, as the commander of a division, he contributed to the victory by his circumspect and resolute action. He was present, but not actually engaged, at the fight at Rossbach, with all its astonishing incidents, when Frederick by sheer good generalship defeated the French, his own army suffering but a trifling loss. The month of November, 1757, marks the turning point in his career. The defeat of Cumberland at Hastenbeck in the previous July, and the shameful compact he concluded at Kloster Zeven, aroused the indignation of the allied nations. George the Second gave emphatic expression of his disapproval of the conduct of his son, who, in consequence, resigned all his appointments, and Frederick declared to Ferdinand that "any one of us is worth four of him."

George the Second asked that Ferdinand should command the Hanoverian and Prussian Army in North-West Germany, which was then holding the line of the Weser and protecting Hanover, and Frederick consented, as it was of the utmost importance to him that his flank should be secure. Supported by the knowledge that he had the confidence of both sovereigns, Ferdinand took up at Stade, with tact and thoroughness, the leadership of the army with which he was to gain lasting renown. His first and most difficult task was to raise the morale of Cumberland's beaten army, and then to re-organize it, and, by an addition to its numbers, to make it equal to the strain he was soon to put upon it. His immediate care was to inspire his troops with confidence in himself as a leader. First, studiously considering the material-wants of his men, he gave them next a taste of the pleasures of success.

Within six weeks of his assumption of the command, he surprised the French in their cantonments and drove them across the Rhine, and, by the end of March, 1758, he had chased the French out of Germany. In June, 1758, at Crefeld, he attacked the French under Clermont, and in a strong position. Dividing his relatively small force into three columns, he made three simultaneous attacks which forced out the French, with a loss of four thousand men. The tactics were risky, for the failure of one column would have wrecked probably the whole plan. In this year, he was raised by Frederick to the rank of field-marshal, "as a proof of my friendship and of my gratitude for the distinguished services you have so well performed for the common cause."

Not the least of Ferdinand's trials arose from the strange mixture of his army, which was composed of Prussians, Hanoverians, Hessians, Brunswickers, and men of Gotha and Schaumberg-Lippe. To these were added, in August, 1758, the British division of eight thousand men, who, aware that their country was paying for the support of others, and inflated with their insular pride and the belief in their superiority as fighting-men, considered that they were justified in expecting special treatment. All this made the task of the urbane Ferdinand of Brunswick a heavy one, and the noble features of the big, powerful, handsome prince were often wrested from their naturally serene aspect by the strain of the bickerings within his army.

The impatience of Frederick the Great, his short, caustically-worded notes, had more than once brought Ferdinand to the thought of resigning his command: but, the extreme exactness of the king in relation to all who served him, whether it was his brother. Prince Henry "the faultless general", or generals of less note, reconciled Ferdinand to the sometimes exasperating sternness of the "Great Master", whom he so faithfully served. And so, his untiring energy, soldierly spirit, and military genius carried him triumphantly to the victories of Crefeld, Minden, Warburg, Vellinghausen, Wilhelmsthal, and Amöneburg. He had beaten five Marshals of France, who had on all occasions outnumbered him. In the last entry in Ferdinand's war diary, made on November 23rd, is seen the humility of the man—

> This is the end of a campaign in which I had to fight with friend (so called) and enemy. Providence has manifested itself during the course of this campaign by the powerful protection which it has vouchsafed me. His holy name be glorified. The term of my rude career was five years.

George the Second conferred upon Ferdinand the Order of the Garter. The investiture was performed in camp, the king having constituted the Marquis of Granby, and the Garter principal King of Arms, plenipotentiaries for investing his Serene Highness. Peace was declared, and, through the Speaker, the House of Commons sent a letter of thanks to the "Victor of Minden", and voted for him an annual pension of £3,000, to which the king added £1,200.

Early in 1763, Ferdinand paid a visit to Frederick at Potsdam, and he accompanied the king to Westphalia in June of that year, when they visited the battlefields of Minden, Warburg, and Vellinghausen. At the conclusion of the war, Ferdinand resumed his governorship of Magdeburg, and there, in 1766, the king held an inspection and review of the troops. During this visit their relationship became strained. The cause of this rupture of a friendship that should have ended with life only, was probably Frederick's impetuosity in speaking. He had the power of lashing people into fury, and this made for him many enemies in high places. It must be sorrowfully recorded that Ferdinand of Brunswick resigned his rank, positions, and appointments in the Prussian Army, and in November he became a field-marshal in the Austrian service, and the colonel of a Bohemian regiment.

When war was declared between England and the American Colonies, George the Third offered Ferdinand the command of the army, which he declined. How the possibility of his entertaining such a proposal could ever have crossed the mind of the king, with the knowledge that Lord George Germain was a Minister of State, is, even at this distance of time, difficult to understand. Perhaps the king was swayed by the last speech in Parliament of the great Pitt, now Lord Chatham, who, as he had done in 1758, so again in 1776, recommended, with all the fervour of his burning eloquence, that Ferdinand of Brunswick should command the Army of England.

A reconciliation between Frederick the Great and Ferdinand was brought about later, but it seems to have been domestic in its character. Between the years 1772 and 1782, Frederick visited Ferdinand at least four times at his estate at Vechelde. Two such men, closely related, could never have lost all affection for one another. In a testamentary paper, dated January 8th, 1769, Frederick bequeathed "to the prince, my brother-in-law, whom I always esteemed, a tobacco-box set with diamonds, and a measure of raw wine." From 1784, Ferdinand began to show signs of failing health, and he contracted a pulmonary disease which ended fatally on July 3rd, 1792. He survived Frederick the Great by six years.

Ferdinand of Brunswick is one of the most revered masters of the school of Frederick the Great. In the Prussian histories, it is recorded that he showed in his high office all the virtues by which men are governed and events are influenced, such as patience, justice, candour, politeness, method, and sincere moderation.

The picture following is an illustration of a parade of the Second Life-Guards, with Frederick the Great on horseback in the centre. The Crown Prince, afterwards Frederick William the Second, General Ramin, General Ziethen, and an *aide-de-camp* follow, all mounted.

A Parade before Frederick the Great

CHAPTER 11

# The Hereditary Prince, Afterwards, the Duke of Brunswick

The hero of the Seven Years' War most popular with the English people was Charles William Ferdinand of Brunswick, commonly known as the hereditary prince. He was only 22 years of age at the beginning of the war, and his youth and enterprise, with his dash as a cavalry leader, fascinated the public imagination. Tall and dignified, with an open, pleasing countenance, his presence seemed to shed a halo of romance around substantial military achievements. He was the eldest son of the eldest sister of Frederick the Great, and his father was the Duke of Brunswick, elder brother of Prince Ferdinand. He was the favourite nephew of his two uncles, and he was beloved by all with whom he came in contact.

In his first battle, he drew upon himself the attention of two armies. At Hastenbeck, the last defeat of the incompetent Cumberland, the hereditary prince gained great honour by recapturing the central battery, when he was acclaimed at once as a leader capable of turning the fate of a battle. Frederick said that "Nature designed him for a hero". He was conspicuous in the actions and battles of Gohfeld, Warburg, Kirch Dinker, Fulda, Kloster Kampen, and in many minor affairs.

In 1764, the hereditary prince came on a visit to England, where he spent thirteen days, and was received by the people with the heartiest enthusiasm. He came, in the glory of heroism, to be wedded to an English princess.

The king and the court, who were not in favour of heroes, gave him a reception in marked contrast with that given him by the nation. He was received with bare civility. Every effort was made to prevent him from meeting Pitt, and the leaders of the Opposition: but, his insistence defeated his opponents. George the Third, however, had his revenge—small, petty, and undignified: but, he had it. He forbade the royal servants to wear their new liveries at the prince's wedding. The marked neglect of the king, and the cold reception accorded to his illustrious guest, were resented by the people, whose warmth in consequence was greatly intensified.

In the Bavarian War of Succession of 1779, the prince commanded an entrenched position in the mountains near Troppau, whence the Austrian commander failed to dislodge him. The following year, he succeeded his father as Duke of Brunswick, and from that year, until 1806, he governed his country wisely, and with liberality far in advance of his age, being esteemed the pattern ruling prince in Europe.

His domestic life was not a happy one. His two eldest sons were imbecile, the third blind, and the fourth, with whom his father was not on good terms, was "Brunswick's fated Chieftain" who fell at Quatre Bras. His eldest daughter married miserably in Russia, while the youngest daughter, Caroline, became the unfortunate consort of George the Fourth. Letters written by the latter, who is described as Princess Caroline of Wales, wife of the prince regent and afterwards his queen, were printed in *The Globe* of May 30th, 1813, and recently, on the same day, one hundred years later, they were reprinted in that paper. The prince had refused to see his wife ever since the first year of their marriage, and, writing to him a bitter letter of complaint, she says, "I have been declared innocent: I will not submit to be treated as guilty."

At the present time, if the *Kaiser* is not the founder he is, at all events, the organiser of modern Germany. In 1913, his only daughter, Princess Victoria Louise, married the son of the Duke of Cumberland, and his triumphant diplomacy was crowned with success on November 3rd, 1913, when Prince Ernest Augustus of Cumberland, described in the *Almanach de Gotha* for 1914, as Prince Ernest Auguste, Duc de Brunswick et de Lunebourg, and his bride, entered Brunswick, as the duke and duchess. From that moment, there was removed any ill-feeling between the House of Hanover and the German throne. This event was of special interest for the British nation with its friendly and intimate connection with Brunswick; for, the younger branch of Brunswick-Lüneburg, namely, that of Hanover, founded for Great Britain her present dynasty.

In the *Gazette* of July 17th, 1914, it was officially announced that King George V. had been pleased to declare and ordain that the children born to their Royal Highnesses the Duke and Duchess of Brunswick and Lüneburg shall at all times hold and enjoy the style and attribute of "Highness" with their titular dignity of prince or princess prefixed to their respective Christian names, or with any titles of honour which may belong to them; and, that the designation of the said children shall be "a prince (or princess) of the United Kingdom of Great Britain and Ireland".

A son was born to their Royal Highnesses in March, 1914.

Until 1792, the public life of the hereditary prince was one of unqualified success. His fame was European, and, by competent judges, he was held to be a really great man.

Yet, even in early life, he showed a tendency to call in too many counsellors, and a proneness to follow the last opinion. His feeling towards his two uncles was one of reverential affection, and he rendered to them implicit and unquestioning obedience. To the end, this had an unconscious influence when he was brought into personal contact with the reigning sovereign, and, both for Germany and for the prince, the consequences were disastrous. Personally, he was daily in the pillory of self-inspection, and, as years went on, his pedantic exactness in examining the most minute detail, and in turning every subject inside out, made it difficult for him to arrive at any decision; so, that, he was unable to give a direct answer "yes" or "no".

Nevertheless, so high was he held in estimation, that, in 1792, he was invited to Paris, where he was offered the command of the French Army, which invitation he wisely declined. He loathed the ideas of the émigrés, and, though from his liberal views he was regarded as a democratic prince, he had a deeply-rooted aversion to the democracy. He deprecated as an illusion the possible invasion of France, and he explained to a French envoy that, if he were to attempt to invade that country, he would place two armies on the frontier in impregnable positions, and then allow the armies of the Republic to shatter themselves against them.

At the same time, at the command of the King of Prussia, for whose abilities he had a profound contempt, he drew up a plan for the invasion of France. In deference to the opinion of the king, he diverted the army from the line of advance upon which he had decided, although it was unquestionably the best. This has been described as an act of madness, and its direct consequence was the defeat at Valmy on September 20th, 1794, which showed the French Republic and their enemies the power of the French Army. Goethe, who was present at the battle as a spectator, was asked by Prussian officers in their consternation, when all was over, what he thought of the engagement, and he replied, "from this place, and from this day forth, commences a new era in the world's history, and you can all say you were present at its birth".

His retreat was a masterpiece of skill, and he recaptured Frankfurt, occupying a very strong position on the heights of Kiltrichon near Pirmasens, He inflicted a signal defeat on the French. In this battle, the Duke led the storming columns against the heights of Kiltrichon. He wanted to pursue the French, but the incapable Sovereign again intervened, and the fruits of victory were thrown away. To Massenbach he wrote:

> We could have conquered France, but we are making her all powerful, and we shall go under.

While in winter-quarters, by a series of feigned movements, he induced Hoche to attack him, and this developed into the three days' Battle of Kaiserlautern, fought on November 28th, 29th and 30th. On the second day, the duke took the offensive, and the long struggle ended in the total defeat of the French. Again, the king would not allow him to follow up the victory.

Disgusted and disappointed, he wrote to the successor of Frederick the Great, on January 9th, 1794,:

> Suspicion, egotism, and a spirit of cabal, have in two campaigns destroyed the result of every measure. . . . prudence requires, honour demands, resignation.

And, forthwith, he left the army. Pirmasens and Kaiserlautern were real victories. He failed only on the moral side. He had the strength to save Germany, and, had he exerted that strength, he would have been supported by the powers opposed to France. That he failed to do so is the reproach that must stand against his name.

The plan of the campaign was altered at the instance of the king, and, rather than consent to its alteration, the duke should have immediately resigned. With the arrival of the king all unity of command disappeared.

The Battle of Auerstädt was fought on the same date as that of Jena, October 14th, 1806. The Duke of Brunswick was then in his 71st year, but showed the activity and keenness of a young man. He personally reconnoitred the ground and the enemy's movements. The roar of the guns was the only tonic which he needed to restore within him his soldierly instinct. He was at once a man of action ready to meet every emergency in the battlefield. At a glance, he fixed the key of the position on some low hills that commanded Hassenhausen. His dispositions were made up by mid-day. He led the attack on the centre of the village. The attack on the French was being pressed home, and the low hills were being occupied, when the duke was grievously wounded.

To encourage the troops who were in front of Hassenhausen, he placed himself at their head, and at that moment a shot passed through his nose, grazing both his eyes and blinding him. Even after this desperate wound, and with his face bound-up, he remounted: but, the effort was beyond human endurance, and he was carried off the field. The incapacity of the king was now supreme, he could neither command the army himself, nor nominate anyone else to command it. Had the duke not been wounded, the French would have been annihilated; whereas, they won the fight.

In the hour of defeat and disaster, the Duke of Brunswick was a great man, but, from Hastenbach to Auerstädt, he was a hero.

He died on November 10th, 1806, at Ottensen, where he was buried.

Chapter 12

# The Minden Regiments

The Suffolk Regiment.
Regimental District No. 13.

The details of great national events are embodied in the little-known histories of the regiments of the British Army. The deeds that won the Empire, and handed it down to our days, are set forth in their volumes, in plain, soldierly words, and it would be of inestimable value, in the promotion of patriotism, were schoolchildren taught the histories of their County-Regiments, even though the ancient bugbear of a Standing-Army, that has come down from the revolutionary days of 1642, should arise. Ignorance is preferred frequently to knowledge, when the latter is antagonistic to personal interests, and people think in an individual, rather than in a national or an imperial sense, imperialism and militarism being confused as synonymous terms. If the schools were to teach history in its truest form, reference should be made to our regimental histories, in order to appreciate the marvellous work which has been accomplished by our army, with its continuous and unbroken record since 1661, or, taking the date of the Grenadier Guards, since 1656.

At the Restoration, Charles the Second disbanded the Army of the Commonwealth. Those dark-visaged warriors, who received their new sovereign on Hounslow Heath in sullen silence, inspired the king with anything but feelings of confidence.

The army, as we know it, was created by degrees, and as it was needed, to meet some national, or dynastic, emergency. Thus, many of our regiments are associated with great historical events, and this applies to four of the six Minden Regiments. The crisis produced by the Rebellion of Monmouth brought about the first addition to the army to which it is necessary to refer. Monmouth's fate was sealed by his defeat at Sedgemoor; but, James the Second, with the fear of a more formidable opponent before his eyes, increased the standing Army by twelve regiments of cavalry and nine regiments of infantry.

One of the latter was the 12th, or East Suffolk, Regiment. The 12th Regiment was made the test-regiment by James the Second, and all its officers and men, except about a dozen, laid down their arms, refusing to pledge themselves to accept the King's Declaration of Indulgence; and now, after a lapse of more than two centuries, history nearly repeated itself, not as regards a sovereign or a dynasty, but as regards a great political party, had not the situation been saved by the action of an incautious general.

When James the Second was deposed, the army passed over to William the Third and under this sovereign, in 1690, it saw its first active engagement at the Battle of the Boyne, followed in quick succession by engagements at Athlone, Aughrim, Waterford and Limerick. Variety of scene was not wanting in the 17th and 18th Centuries. In 1694 and 1695, the 12th Regiment was fighting in Flanders, whence it went to the West Indies. In 1708, it had the good fortune to serve under Marlborough at the Siege of Lisle.

The 12th fought at Dettingen in 1743, when George the Second was present, and this was the last battle at which an English king commanded in person. At Fontenoy, where a sanguinary effort was made by Cumberland to take a heavily entrenched camp, the losses of the 12th exceeded those of any other corps engaged, and it was honoured by being one of four regiments mentioned in the duke's despatches. Such were the distinctions of the 18th century. In the "Seven Years' War", at the Battle of Minden, on the right of the first line of the British Infantry, the 12th bore the full brunt of the charges of the French Cavalry and of the storm of artillery and musket-fire, and, as Prince Ferdinand of Brunswick declared, "gained immortal glory". Its casualties in killed, wounded and missing, were 19 officers and 283 men. It was present also at Warburg, Vellinghausen and Wilhelmstahl.

Sixteen years elapsed, and the 12th earned distinction again at Gibraltar, during the siege of the fortress, which lasted five years, from 1779 to 1783. It was one of the three regiments that made the famous sortie on November 26th, 1781, when the Spanish works, of which the erection had cost two million pounds, were destroyed. This siege showed the stern, resolute character of the British soldier, and here the 17th won the "Castle and Key" which are the regimental badge.

Under Sir Charles Grey, the flank companies took part in the capture of Port Royal and Guadeloupe. The deadly nature of service in the West Indies in the 18th century can be estimated by the fact that only three survivors of these two companies rejoined the regiment.

From 1796 to 1817, the 12th served in India, and in the Mauritius. The long Napoleonic struggle, no doubt, was the cause of this prolonged service in the East. In 1799, it took part in the Mysore campaign, being present at the action fought at Mallavelly, and at the storming of Seringapatam. It was the Light Company of the 12th that intercepted and shot the Sultan Tippoo Sahib and his guard, as they were entering the fortress. It became necessary to bring the Rajah of Travancore into subjection, and, though supported only by *sepoys*, the r2th defeated the Travancore army at Quilon and Cochin. Their service in India was varied by an expedition which captured the Islands of Burbon and Mauritius in the Indian Ocean.

From India, the 12th was transferred to Ireland in 1817, and it was not engaged again on active service until 1851-3, when it fought against the Kaffirs in South Africa, and, ten years later, against the Maories in New Zealand. In 1878-80, it was in Afghanistan, and, ten years later, it took part in the Hazara Black Mountain Expedition.

In 1899, when England was at war with the Boers, the Suffolk Regiment was sent to South Africa, and comprised part of the army, then in Cape Colony under General French, to resist the Boer invasion. At Colesburg, it met with a repulse in making a midnight-attack upon a Boer position. In this unfortunate affair, it lost 11 officers, including the Commanding Officer, and 150 men. The Suffolk subsequently fought in various parts of South Africa, with the entire confidence of the generals under whom they served.

This brief outline of the services of this "Minden Regiment" may be concluded by mentioning the fact that between 1864 and 1903, four officers of the "Suffolks" won the Victoria Cross.

The Suffolk Regiment bears upon its colours. The Castle and Key, superscribed "Gibraltar, 1779-83", with the motto, "*Montis Insignia Calpe*", underneath. The battle-honours are Dettingen, Minden, Seringapatam, India, South Africa, 1851-2-3, New Zealand, Afghanistan, 1878-80, South Africa, 1899-1902.

## The Lancashire Fusiliers.
### Regimental District No. 20.

The dark forebodings of James the Second were soon realised, and

General von Wangenheim

the landing at Torbay of the Prince of Orange, with an army, brought about a bloodless revolution. On reaching Exeter, William sanctioned an augmentation of the army and the immediate raising of three regiments, one of them being the 20th. Recruited in and about Exeter, it was given the name of the East Devonshire Regiment in 1782, and nominally Devonshire was its home until 1881, when it became the Lancashire Fusiliers. Famous soldiers have commanded it. Under Gustavus Hamilton it fought at the Boyne, Athlone, Aughrim and Limerick. Portugal and the West Indies absorbed it during the brilliant campaigns of Marlborough. Dettingen, Culloden and Fontenoy are names that need only be repeated to show that it hurried from one field of action to another. For nine years, it was under the personal command of Wolfe, and by him it was brought to a state of efficiency hitherto unknown in the British Army.

At the Battle of Minden, the 20th was on the right of the second line of British infantry, and its losses exceeded those of any other corps engaged, in fact they were so heavy that Prince Ferdinand by a special order struck the regiment off duty. On the following day, this order was cancelled by the announcement that Kingsley's Regiment, at its own request, resumed its duty. There is a tradition that the survivors of the regiment, as they passed through some gardens near the town of Minden, plucked roses and stuck them in their caps. This tradition has been accepted by every succeeding generation and, on August 1st, the anniversary of the battle, roses are worn by the whole Regiment. The red rose, moreover, is the badge of the County of Lancaster. The 20th took part in the actions fought at Warburg, Vellinghausen, Kloster Kampen and Wilhelmsthal. The grenadiers of the army were commanded by Colonel Beckwith, and one battalion of grenadiers by Major Maxwell, both officers of the 20th.

It is of interest to record that Ensign Lawrence carried one of the colours of the 20th in the Battle of Minden, and that he was the great-grandfather of Major-General (then, Brigadier-General) Fry, C.V.O., C.B., who in 1909 commanded the East Lancashire Territorial Division.

Moreover, Captain C. L. Lutyens, an officer of the 20th Regiment, living at The Cottage, Thursley, Godalming, is related to the German General von Wangenheim, the space between whose Hanoverian Division on the left and the rest of Prince Ferdinand's line attracted the attention of the French Marshal Contades, and induced him to make the advance, which was one of the first moves of the battle.

Captain Lutyens, who was 85 years of age on January 15th, 1914, provides an illustration of historical bridging; for, three generations of his family, covering a period of 155 years, connect him with the Battle of Minden. The father of Captain Lutyens was for a long time in the commissariat in the Peninsula, and died leaving two sons, and a daughter who died young. Captain Lutyens was a son by a second marriage. He left home when he was nineteen years of age, and never saw his father again. The portrait of General von Wangenheim, reproduced in this book, was painted by an artist named Braun. It is in the possession of Captain Lutyens and, with it, are portraits of Madame von Wangenheim and of the wife of her stepson Captain Lutyens. The widowed Madame von Wangenheim lived in London with her and her husband, and the Royal Dukes of the time used to visit her.

The glories of the "Seven Years' War" were not repeated in the fratricidal struggle with the American Colonists, but soldiers never fought better than those of Burgoyne's small army at Freeman's Farm and Bemus Heights. The surrender at Saratoga gave America her independence.

The 20th bore its share in the acquisition of the West Indies, and, after one short campaign in St. Domingo, less than 100 men returned to England. Within three years of its return, the 20th was fighting against the combined forces of the French and Dutch in Holland, and, at the Battle of Krabbendam, it held the salient point during a critical turn of the battle. It fought again in the two battles of Egmont-op-Zee.

The good fortunes of the 20th followed it to Italy, where, in 1806, it took a conspicuous part in the defeat of the French at the Battle of Maida, which was the first check administered by the British to Napoleon's soldiers. England was now in the throes of the Napoleonic struggle, and the 20th took its share in the War in the Peninsula, and in the final expulsion of the French from Spain and Portugal. Vimiera, the retreat on and the Battle of Corunna, followed by the Walcheren Expedition, made a sojourn of two years in the South of Ireland necessary for recuperation.

In 1812, it was again on active service with the Army in the Peninsula. It was present at Vittoria, and at all the actions fought on the slopes of the Pyrenees, and, finally, it took part in the invasion of France, and the Battles of Orthes, the Nivelle and Toulouse.

It was permitted to the 20th to watch the last days of Napoleon at St. Helena, and, that they performed there an unpleasant duty with a kindly consideration for the susceptibilities of the illustrious prisoner, is testified by the fact that he made presentations to the two officers who had been brought in personal contact with him, and that he gave to the officers' mess a copy of Cox's *Life of Marlborough*.

Early in the year 1914, the French training-ship *Jeanne d'Arc*, with seventy naval cadets visited Karachi in India, where the 1st Battalion of the Lancashire Fusiliers, under Lieutenant-Colonel H.V. S. Ormond, was stationed. There was a cordial reception by the municipality and by the military, the English soldiers and the French sailors fraternizing together. The French officers were delighted with the Napoleonic relics in the mess, and some of them were quite affected.

A tour of service in India, in the West Indies, and in Canada, filled up the long period of peace between Waterloo and the Crimean War, in which the regiment took part in the Battles of the Alma, Balaclava and the Siege of Sebastopol, and at Inkerman, centred about the Sandbag Battery, it lost more than any other regiment engaged, the Guards alone excepted. Returning to England in 1856, it was after a short interval of one year sent to India, where it took part in the siege and capture of Lucknow, and in other actions, until the Mutiny was suppressed.

In the *Times* of September 6th, 1904, Major-General Sir Owen Tudor Burne drew attention to the connection of the Japanese Army with the Lancashire Fusiliers, and allusion to it is made in *A History of the Lancashire Fusiliers*, by Major B. Smyth, M.V.O. I have now received a letter from a correspondent, who recently made for me some inquiries on the subject, and ascertained the facts from a Japanese gentleman, who himself received military instruction at the Camp in Yokohama, in the far-off days of 1864, when the XX. Regiment was stationed there. He writes:

> The name of my informant is Takashi Masuda, a man of quite exceptional ability, who is now the Managing-Director of the House of Mitsui & Company, the Rothschilds of Japan. Masuda was born in the island of Sado in 1848. His father was a Samurai in the service of the Shogun, and Masuda himself became a cavalry-officer in the same service. Both father and son came to France in 1862 in the retinue of two ambassadors sent by the Shogun's Government. He told me incidentally that two or three members of this Embassy had brought with them suits of Japanese armour, and, by desire of the Emperor Napoleon the

Third, they attended a review of troops clad in this bizarre array. When I arrived in Japan in June, 1866, Yokohama was guarded by the Norfolk Regiment. They had relieved the Lancashire Fusiliers: but, a certain number of the latter remained, with three of their officers, namely. Captain Rochfort, Lieutenant Webster, Lieutenant Harris the musketry-instructor, and Ensign De la Pere Robinson. Of these four officers, Colonels Webster and Robinson are the survivors today, (1914). I remember all these officers, but Webster was the only one whom I actually knew: they left soon after my arrival.

Mr. Harris had devoted himself to training some officers and troops of the Shogun Iyemochi, Masuda among the number. The commander was an officer whose rank corresponded to colonel: his name being Kubota Sentaro. This was undoubtedly the body of troops, two thousand strong, of which you spoke as having been brigaded with our troops on October 20th, 1864, and as wearing their quaint chain-armour, with swords, bows and arrows, as their weapons. I have a clear recollection of having seen a photograph of Sentaro himself taken in his armour. The Shogun Iyemochi died in August, 1866, and the new Shogun Yoshihisa, better known perhaps as Keiki, found himself face to face with the revolt of the Southern Daimios, which resulted in the restoration of the Mikado, and the abolition of the Shogunate. Hostilities were of brief duration, and the fate of the Shogun was decided at the Battle of Fushimi, near Kioto. At this engagement Kubota Sentaro was killed. This was in 1868. In a Japanese History entitled *Kinsé Shiriaku*, he is described as Kubota Bizen-no-kami, that is. Lord of Bizen—he had evidently been ennobled either by Iyemochi or Keiki—, and as formerly commander of the Japanese garrison at Yokohama.

Keiki, the last *Shogun*, died this year (1914) in Tokio. I think he was about 74 years of age. After his defeat, he soon became a loyal subject of the emperor, when he was given the rank of prince, by the emperor. Masuda said he was 'A very happy old gentleman.'

After an interval from active service in the field of forty years, the 2nd Battalion took part in the Battle of Khartoum, and in the final defeat and overthrow of the Dervish power in the Sudan. In 1900, after the outbreak of the war in South Africa, it served with the Natal Army, under General Buller, in the operations for the relief of Ladysmith. At Spion Kop, on January 24th, 1900, it suffered heavily, its casualties in killed and wounded being 12 officers and 225 men. It served until the end of the War in South Africa.

The Lancashire Fusiliers bear upon their colours. The Sphinx superscribed "Egypt", The Red Rose, and the motto, "*Omnia audax*", which may be translated, "daring in all things". The battle-honours are Dettingen, Minden, Egmont-op-Zee, Maida, Vimiera, Corunna, Vittoria, Pyrenees, Orthes, Toulouse, Peninsula, Alma, Inkerman, Sevastopol, Lucknow, Khartoum, South Africa, 1899-1902, Relief of Ladysmith.

## THE ROYAL WELSH FUSILIERS.
## REGIMENTAL DISTRICT NO. 33.

The 23rd Regiment, or the Welsh Fusiliers, now the Royal Welsh Fusiliers, one of the regiments added to the army by William the Third, came into existence in the year 1689. It was raised in Wales, and, throughout its distinguished career, it has been a Welsh Regiment. Its first fighting-service was under William in Ireland. In 1694 and 1695, it was in active service in Flanders, and its first battle-honour is "Namur": this was the largest operation in war of William, and it cost him 12,000 men. The regiment took part in Marlborough's Campaign, including the celebrated march to the Danube and the Battles of Blenheim, Ramillies, Oudenarde and Malplaquet, names of which the British Army has cause to be proud. After the peace of Utrecht, it had conferred upon it the distinctive honour of becoming the "Prince of Wales Own Royal Regiment of Welsh Fusiliers". In 1715, it was engaged in Scotland in suppressing the rebellion in favour of the Pretender, and it took part in the Battle of Sheriffmuir. When England became involved in the War of the Austrian Succession, the 23rd fought, in 1743, at Dettingen under George the Second. Fontenoy and Culloden were its military services in 1745.

The surrender of Port Mahon in Minorca, after a siege of 70 days, cast no reflection on the honour of the 23rd, or of the other three regiments, who gallantly defended it, sacrificed as they were by the neglect of the government at home. It was for the failure at Minorca that Admiral Byng paid the penalty with his life.

"The Seven Years' War" brought the Welsh Fusiliers the honours of Minden, Warburg, Kloster Kampen, Vellinghausen, Wilhelmsthal and Amöneburg.

In the war with the American Colonists, the 23rd took part in the battle of Bunker's Hill, and they had subsequently the unusual experience of serving as marines on board the fleet commanded by the gallant Admiral Lord Howe. They continued to serve against the colonists, and took part in the action of Guildford Court Home. The regiment was one of those that defended Yorktown, and it was included in the terms of capitulation, remaining prisoners of war until the independence of the United States was declared in January, 1783.

It was then on home service for eleven years, 1783-94, and it went to the West Indies in the last-named year.

After two years' service in St. Domingo, it returned to England a mere skeleton, in 1796. Under Sir Ralph Abercromby, it fought against the French Republican troops in Holland, where it won the honour "Egmont-op-Zee." It formed part of the Expedition to Egypt under Sir Ralph Abercromby.

The Welsh Fusiliers contributed to the defeat of Napoleon, beginning with the retreat of Corunna and ending with Waterloo, and, in the meantime, they took part in the victories of Albuera, forming with the 7th the famous "Fusilier Brigade" whose services are so well narrated by Napier, Badajoz, Salamanca, Vittoria, Pyrenees, Nivelle, Orthes and Toulouse. The Crimean War brought to an end the forty years of peace between the great nations: in the first fight, the Battle of the Alma, the 23rd distinguished themselves especially at the storming of the "Great Redoubt", and their losses were proportionately heavy. They were at Inkerman and the Siege of Sebastopol. After a brief interval, the Welsh Fusiliers were in India, serving under Field-Marshal Lord Clyde at the siege and capture of Lucknow, and in subsequent operations.

The Ashantee War in 1873, with the capture of Coomassie, under Sir Garnet Wolseley, and the Burmah War of 1885, kept this distinguished Regiment experienced in actual warfare.

The Welsh Fusiliers formed part of the army under General Buller which relieved Ladysmith, and it served throughout the South African Campaign until its close in 1902.

A detachment of the regiment was at Pekin in 1900 to secure the Consulates, and this is the last honour borne on the colours.

In the Crimea, three officers and three non-commissioned officers won the Victoria Cross.

There is one distinguishing mark that the officers and staff-sergeants of the Royal Welsh Fusiliers have been permitted to wear, namely, the "Flash", which is a knot of black ribbon worn at the back of the neck on the collar of the tunic. The 23rd were the last regiment in the army who wore the powdered hair and pig-tail, and they retained the ribbon in imitation of the queue-bag.

The Royal Welsh Fusiliers bear upon their colours, The plume of the Prince of Wales. In the first and fourth corners the Rising Sun; in the second corner the Red Dragon; in the third corner the White Horse with motto, "*Nec aspera terrent*". The Sphinx, superscribed "Egypt". The battle-honours are Namur, 1695, Blenheim, Ramillies, Oudenarde, Malplaquet, Dettingen, Minden, Corunna, Martinique, 1809, Albuhera, Badajoz, Salamanca, Vittoria, Pyrenees, Nivelle, Orthes, Toulouse, Peninsula, Waterloo, Alma, Inkerman, Sevastopol, Lucknow, Ashantee, Burma, 1885-87, South Africa, 1899-1902, Relief of Ladysmith, Pekin, 1900.

## THE KING'S OWN SCOTTISH BORDERERS.
### REGIMENTAL DISTRICT NO. 25.

The Earl of Leven and other Scottish adherents of William the Third raised in Edinburgh in March, 1689, a regiment of 1,000 men, and tradition says that this was accomplished in the short space of four hours. The fighting qualities of the new regiment were soon put to the test. Graham of Claverhouse at the head of the Highland Clans, espoused the cause of James the Second. General Mackay commanded the army of William. The two armies met in the Pass of Killiecrankie on July 27th, 1689. Mackay was defeated, only two regiments making any show of a fight, and one of these was the King's Own Scottish Borderers. The regiment went from Scotland to Ireland, where it took part in the operations against King James.

It fought at Steinkirk in 1692, and at Landen in 1694. In the latter action, the cowardice of the Dutch Horse brought about the defeat of the Confederate Army. At the siege of Namur, the King's Own Scottish Borderers, by the explosion of one of the enemy's mines, lost 20 officers and 500 men. The Fortress fell to William, but at the great sacrifice of 12,000 men. It fought the Jacobites at Sheriffmuir in 1715. In 1727, the Regiment, besieged in Gibraltar from February to June, beat off 20,000 Spaniards. At Fontenoy, the King's Own Scottish Borderers suffered heavily, losing no less than 206 officers and men. In this battle, although it was a hopeless contest under a commander of such moderate ability as the Duke of Cumberland, who had as his opponent a general of the eminence of Marshal Saxe, the French held a fortified position, and the British were sacrificed by the Dutch who refused to obey orders.

The 25th was one of the six Minden Regiments, being on the left of the second line in the brigade of General Kingsley. At Warburg, Kloster Kampen, Vellinghausen and Wilhelmsthal, they bore their share of the fighting.

In 1782, for the second time, they were engaged in defending Gibraltar against the joint efforts of France and Spain, and garrisoned it afterwards for eleven years, only returning home in 1793. In 1793, they acted as marines, and in this service they were doubly fortunate, for they captured a vessel valued at one million pounds sterling, which gave them a rich harvest of prize-money, and they were engaged in Lord Howe's glorious victory over the French on June 1st, 1794. A detachment of the regiment was present at the siege of Toulon, when Lieutenant Napoleon Bonaparte of the French artillery was wounded. In 1799, the King's Own Scottish Borderers added Egmont-op-Zee to their battle-honours, and two years later they were under Sir Ralph Abercromby when the French were driven finally out of Egypt. Eight years elapsed before the Borderers were again on active service. In 1809, they took part in the capture of Martinique and also of Guadeloupe. In 1814 and 1815, they were serving in Holland. Insurrection in Cape Colony and in Canada afforded the 25th the only active service between the year 1809 and the year 1878, when it took part in the Afghan campaign. In 1888, the Borderers were in the Eastern Sudan defending Suakim against the Dervishes, helping to defeat them at Gemaizah.

The varied service of a British Regiment is illustrated by that of the Borderers. The Cape, Canada, Eastern Sudan, Afghanistan, China, Lushai, Chitral Relief Force, Tirah Campaign, are names following each other in the order in which the regiment was engaged. In the Tirah Campaign, they lost four officers and 32 men killed.

In the Boer War of 1899-1902, the Borderers bore much of the heat and burden of the campaign. In the Orange Free State and the Transvaal their total casualties were 11 officers, and 126 non-commissioned officers and men killed, and 5 officers and 90 non-commissioned officers and men wounded. One officer won the Victoria Cross.

The King's Own Scottish Borderers bear upon their colours, The Castle of Edinburgh, with the motto "*Nisi Dominus frustra*". In the first and fourth corners the Royal Crest, with the motto "*In Veritate Religionis confido*". In the second and third corners the White Horse, with "*Nee aspera terrent*". The Sphinx, superscribed "Egypt". The battle-honours are Namur, 1695, Minden, Egmont-op-Zee, Martinique, 1809, Afghanistan, 1878-80, Chitral, Tirah, South Africa, 1900-02, Paardeborg.

## THE HAMPSHIRE REGIMENT.
### REGIMENTAL DISTRICT NO. 37.

This regiment was raised in Ireland by Colonel Meredith, afterwards Marlborough's adjutant-general, in 1702, and it was given the name of the North Hampshire Regiment in 1782. In two years and three months from that date, it fought under Marlborough at Blenheim, and, remaining with Marlborough's Army, it took its part in the Battles of Ramillies, Oudenarde and Malplaquet. Like all the Minden Regiments, with the exception of the Yorkshire Light Infantry, it fought under George the Second at Dettingen, in 1743.

It formed part of the British contingent that went to Germany in 1758, and served in the Seven Years' War. It was one of the six infantry regiments that destroyed the French cavalry at Minden, being the centre regiment of the first line. The sixty French squadrons were shattered by "the immortal six", a deed that calls forth as much admiration today, (1914), as it did upwards of 150 years ago. As a single battalion, that is before it was joined to the 67th Regiment, the 37th, the Minden Regiment, had three honours.

In 1761, it took part in the capture of Belle Isle off the Brittany coast, and it took part in the Portuguese Campaign of 1762. Thirty-three years later the regiment distinguished itself in the battle fought near Tournay, when the French lost 6,000 in killed and wounded.

It fought through the whole war of the American Rebellion. It garrisoned Gibraltar, 1811-14. The Second Battalion served under Graham in Holland in 1814. It was one of those regiments that held detached positions in Spain, and, therefore, it did not share in the victories won by Wellington, but its services were recognised by the honour "Peninsula" being placed upon its colours.

It served honourably in the Indian Mutiny, 1857-58.

In 1904, the regiment had the exceptional experience of having five companies serving in Arabia, and three companies in Somaliland in East Africa, at the same time, the Somaliland detachment taking a distinguished part in the defeat of the Mullah at Jidballi, and also in the storming of Illig.

In the following list of honours, "Barrosa", and from "Taku Forts" to "Burma, 1885-87", inclusive, belong to the 67th and not to the old 37th of Minden days.

The Hampshire Regiment bears upon its colours. The Royal Tiger, superscribed "India". The battle-honours are Blenheim, Ramillies, Oudenarde, Malplaquet, Dettingen, Minden, Tournay, Barrosa, Peninsula, Taku Forts, Pekin, Charasiah, Kabul, 1879, Afghanistan, 1878-80, Burma, 1885-87, South Africa, 1900-02, Paardeberg.

## THE KING'S OWN (YORKSHIRE LIGHT INFANTRY).
### REGIMENTAL DISTRICT NO. 51.

The certainty of a war with France caused a large increase in the army in 1755. Twelve regiments were added to the establishment, and one of these was the 51st, which was established at first in Exeter, and then, in the same year, transferred to Yorkshire. A public meeting was held in Leeds in March, 1756, at which all present pledged themselves to assist in providing His Majesty with a regiment which, in point of numbers and character of the men, should be worthy of the county. Within the short space of one month, there was presented to His Majesty a regiment of 800 men who agreed to serve for three years, or for as long a time as the country was at war or needed their services. It was raised eighty years after the raising of the 12th, 20th, 23rd and 25th Regiments.

The 51st went to Germany in 1758, when it formed part of the British division of the allied armies under Prince Ferdinand of Brunswick. At Minden, it was in the centre of the second line, sharing the glories of the victory. It served throughout the campaign and returned to England at the conclusion of the war.

In 1771, the regiment was ordered to Minorca, where it remained for eleven years. It assisted to garrison Fort St. Phillip, which was besieged by a French and Spanish force of 14,000 men, and, when the fort capitulated, there were less than 960 survivors to lay down their arms out of the four battalions of the garrison.

The 51st had the honour of having as one of its officers Sir John Moore, by whom it was commanded from 1794 to 1796. The lustre of his great name remains with the regiment, creating a feeling of pride in every succeeding generation.

The regiment went to India in 1798, two years later proceeding to Ceylon, where it was engaged in the war against the King of Candy in 1803.

In 1808, the 51st was again serving under its former colonel, now

General Sir John Moore, in the retreat on Corunna, and by a special general order, dated May, 1809, the regiment was made a Light Infantry Regiment, in recognition of its gallant, steady and soldierly bearing during the retreat, and especially at Lugo.

In the Peninsular War, it took part in the victories of Fuentes d'Onoro, Badajoz, Salamanca, Vittoria, Pyrenees, Nivelle and Orthes. At Waterloo, it was on the right of the British position, and it assisted in the defence of Hougomont. In 1821, the title of King's Own Light Infantry was conferred upon it, and in 1887, this was changed to the King's Own (Yorkshire Light Infantry).

The long spell of peaceful service was broken in Burmah in 1852, when "Pegu" was added to the list of battle honours. Indian service claimed it twenty-five years later in 1877, when it formed part of the Jowaki Expedition, and it went through the campaign of Afghanistan, 1878-80, including the capture of Ali Masjid. Its second battalion, formerly the 105th Madras Light Infantry, has also an honourable war record.

Four sets of old colours, and recently a fifth set of the 2nd Battalion, of the Yorkshire Light Infantry, are deposited in York Minster. The first set are green, matching the facings of the Regiment at the time, and they were carried at the Battle of Minden. The other colours are blue, since the Yorkshire Light Infantry became a Royal Regiment. All the colours have been deposited in York Minster, including a set carried at Waterloo, with the exception of one set which were burnt at Badajos in the Peninsula.

The last Victoria Cross hero to have the decoration pinned on his breast by Queen Victoria was Private C. Ward of the 2nd Battalion of this regiment. With four others, Private Ward attended at Windsor Castle on a Saturday in December, 1900, and he was the last of the party to be decorated. The queen died in the following January.

The King's Own (Yorkshire Light Infantry) bears upon its colours, The White Rose, with the motto, "*Cede nullis*". The battle-honours are Minden, Corunna, Fuentes d'Onoro, Salamanca, Vittoria, Pyrenees, Nivelle, Orthes, Peninsula, Waterloo, Pegu, Ali Masjid, Afghanistan, 1878-80, Burma, 1885-87, South Africa, 1899-1902, Modder River.

★★★★★★

Referring to the Campaign Honours of the Eighteenth Century, the military correspondent of the *Morning Post*, on January 27th, 1914, wrote:

The grant of 'North America 1763-64', as a regimental honour to the Black Watch and the King's Royal Rifle Corps in this month's Army Orders, serves to draw attention to a singular anomaly. Records of regimental services in the early days of the British Standing Army are often very incomplete, and in many cases, considerable doubt exists as to whether individual corps were, or were not, present at some particular action in the field. For instance, when Sir A. Alison's Committee, some twenty years ago, recommended that a number of regiments should be permitted to inscribe the titles of Marlborough's four principal victories on their colours, the name 'Lille' would have been added in commemoration of what was the greatest siege-triumph of those famous campaigns, had it been possible to ascertain exactly which corps would have been entitled to the distinction.

On the other hand, the contemporary records are almost invariably explicit as to the dates when individual regiments proceeded to a theatre of war, and as to the dates when they quitted it. The consequence is that in cases where it is proposed to grant a distinction, not for a particular combat or siege, but for a set of operations as a whole, there can seldom be any difficulty in enumerating the regiments which can fairly claim it. It is a well-understood principle that no honours ought to be granted for an unsuccessful campaign, and, on that account, no notice is very properly taken even of successful actions fought during the course of the American War of Independence. But, successful campaigns ought surely to be remembered on the insignia of all units which took part in them.

The plan has the merit that it meets the case of corps which may not have enjoyed the good fortune to be present at any of the more important actions of the struggle, but which have nevertheless performed good service, and contributed to secure the success of their side. Several regiments have 'South Africa' (with the date) on their colours, although they show no other distinction in connection with the long-drawn-out struggle which lasted from 1899 to 1902. But, oddly enough, the principle has not hitherto been put in force in connection with the triumphs of the British Army during the Eighteenth Century, and the grant of 'North America, 1763-64,' therefore, marks a distinct step in advance.

At the same time, it seems somewhat strange that the success of the old Royal Americans and the Black Watch over the Red Man should be remembered, when numbers of regiments which fought under Prince Ferdinand in North Germany between 1758 and 1762 have nothing to show for their services. Mr. Fortescue has pronounced Prince Ferdinand to have been the 'greatest commander who led British troops to victory between Marlborough and Wellington', and few who are acquainted with the story of his campaigns and of the influence which they exerted in furthering the cause of Frederick the Great will dispute this verdict.

It is true that the names 'Minden', 'Emsdorf' and 'Wilhelmsthal' have for many years past appeared in the Army List, and that 'Warburg' has recently been added to these. But the fact remains that several regiments were present in the theatre of war and took part in successful engagements there which are at present completely overlooked. The Northumberland Fusiliers alone show the honour 'Wilhelmsthal'—in recognition of exceptionally brilliant services—, although practically the whole of Granby's forces were present on the battlefield. Only the cavalry-regiments that took part in the stirring combat of 'Warburg' display the name on their appointments, and that is perfectly right, as the bulk of the infantry could not get up in time; but for all that, the grenadier-companies of a number of battalions played a very important part in achieving victory.

The very successful action of Kirch Dinker or Vellinghausen in 1761 would certainly not have been ignored had the fight taken place a century later. The proper course, however, would seem to be to leave matters as they are in respect to individual engagements, but to grant 'North Germany', with the date, to all corps that fought under Prince Ferdinand. Those which, in addition to the Minden and Warburg regiments and the 15th Hussars and Northumberland Fusiliers, would thus be enabled to show that they took part in these memorable operations of war, would appear to be the following: the three regiments of Foot Guards (the Guards Brigade only arrived in 1760, after Warburg), the Liverpool Regiment, the Devons, the South Wales Borderers, the West Riding, and the Royal West Kent.

This same principle ought also to be applied to the case of Marlborough's campaign. A number of regiments fought during the first two or three years of the operations in the Low Countries, which were afterwards transferred to the Peninsula. The old 12th Foot (the Suffolks) joined Marlborough for the campaigns of 1708 and 1709, and although not present at either Oudenarde or Malplaquet, they undoubtedly took part in the remarkable action of Wynendale, which contributed so largely to the final success of the Allies at Lille. The '2nd Queen's' owe their motto, '*Pristinoe virtutis memor*' to their staunch defence of Tongres in 1703; yet, they have nothing to show that they served under Marlborough.

The old name 'Flanders' might well be revived in this connection, and the honour, with the date, be granted to all regiments which served in this theatre during the war of the Spanish Succession. The corps which would appear to be entitled to the distinction (in addition to the numerous ones that show 'Blenheim', 'Ramillies', 'Oudenarde', and 'Malplaquet') are the Royal Dragoons, the Queen's, the Norfolks, the Devons, the Suffolks, the Somersets, the Leicestershire, and the Border Regiment.

LORD GEORGE SACKVILLE

CHAPTER 13

# The Charge Against Lord George Sackville

The following account of the charge against Lord George, in relation to his conduct at the Battle of Minden, is taken from the Annual Register, 1760, pages 175 to 178 inclusive:

> A compendious state of the case of Lord George Sackville, as it appears from the trial published by his own direction.

It is corroborated by a book of 224 pages, published by Authority in 1760, entitled *The proceedings of a General Court-Martial, held at the Horse-Guards on Friday the 7th, and continued by several adjournments to Monday the 24th of March, 1760; and of a General Court-Martial held at the Horse-Guards on Tuesday the 25th of March, and continued by several adjournments to Saturday the 5th of April, 1760, upon the Trial of Lord George Sackville*

> The charge against Lord George Sackville is, the disobedience of orders from Prince Ferdinand; his defence is in substance as follows:
> That orders were given, the night before the battle, for the troops to be in readiness at one the next morning; the horses of the cavalry to be then saddled, but not to strike tents or march till further orders; that these orders having been frequently given, for a fortnight before, were not alone sufficient to apprise Lord George of an engagement next morning; that the first notice that Lord George, Lord Granby, and other general-officers, had of an attack, was from the firing of cannon between five and six; that Lord George immediately rose, being waked by

the sound, and rode, from the village where he was quartered, to the head of the cavalry, which was then mounted, and he was there before any other general-officer of the division; that he marched them, though no orders to march had yet reached him, towards a windmill in front; that when he had advanced a considerable distance, he received an order to halt, and wait till he should receive further orders.

That while he remained on or near this ground, the artillery had also marched from its ground, though neither had that received any orders; and Lord George imagining that orders to the artillery had been forgotten, in the hurry usual upon a surprise, he ordered it to advance in front, where it was of signal service.

That Captain Wintzingerode soon after brought him an order *to form a line, as a third line to support the infantry, and advance*; that he said nothing about going *to the left, between trees, or coming out upon a heath,* nor told him where the infantry to be sustained were to be found, but only repeated his order twice in French, which Lord George requested him to do, not from any difficulty he found in comprehending the general intention of the words, but because they were at first expressed indistinctly through hurry; that Lord George supposing that, *to advance*, was *to go forward*, immediately began to execute these orders, by sending an officer to a Saxe Gotha regiment of foot, that obstructed his way in front, to cause it to remove out of his way, thinking it better so to do than to cause our artillery, which obstructed the only other way he could have advanced, to halt; despatching at the same time a second officer to see where the infantry he was to sustain was posted, and a third to reconnoitre the situation of the enemy; that while this was doing, Colonel Ligonier came up with an order *to advance with the cavalry,* in order to profit of a *disorder which appeared in the cavalry of the enemy*; and that neither did he mention, or at least was not heard to mention, any movement *to the left.*

That the Saxe Gotha regiment being by this time removed from the front. Lord George, in obedience to the *concurrent* orders of Captain Wintzingerode and Colonel Ligonier, as he understood them, and as they were understood by his witnesses, ordered the troops to advance *straight forward*; that this could not be more than eight minutes after he had received the order that had been brought by Captain Wintzingerode, because Captain Wintzingerode, as he was riding back from Lord George, met Colonel Fitzroy riding to him very fast; and when Colonel Fitzroy arrived, the troops were in motion; that it appears from all the witnesses, that they could not have been put in motion in much less than eight minutes, as five minutes were given, even by the witnesses for the prosecution, for the Saxe Gotha regiment to move out of his way.

That almost immediately after the troops were in motion, Colonel Fitzroy came up, and brought the *first* orders he *heard* for moving *to the left*, at the same time limiting the movement to the *British* cavalry; that then, being in doubt what to do, he halted; the order that arrived last, by Colonel Fitzroy, not superseding the former order by Colonel Ligonier; as Lord George and those about him understood, both from Fitzroy and Ligonier, that they brought the *same order*, having received it at the same time, and brought it at different times by having taken different routes; that not being able to agree, each earnestly pressing the execution of his own orders.

Lord George took a resolution to go to the prince, who was not far distant. That Colonel Ligonier went forward, and that as Lord George was riding on with Colonel Fitzroy, he perceived the wood on the left more open than he had thought it, which inclined him to think it possible the prince might have ordered him to the left; and Colonel Fitzroy still vehemently pressing the execution of the orders he brought, he sent Captain Smith with orders for the *British Cavalry to move to the left*; the motion *to the left* and the *limitation* of the movement to the *British*, being connected in the same order, and both *peculiar* to that brought by Colonel Fitzroy; that by this means scarce any delay was made even by the difference of orders brought by the two *aides-de-camp*, Captain Smith not having advanced above 200 yards beyond the left of the British Cavalry; the time therefore could only be what he took up in galloping twice that space; that this period includes all the time in which Lord George is supposed to have disobeyed orders, by an unnecessary delay.

The facts upon which the defence is founded are directly and positively contradicted by Captain Wintzingerode, Colonel Sloper, and Colonel Ligonier. Captain Wintzingerode deposed, that upon delivering his orders to Lord George in French, Lord

George *seemed not to understand them*, asked *how that was to be done*; that he then explained them, and made him understand that he was to pass with the cavalry *between the trees* that he saw on the left; that he would then arrive upon a *heath*, where he was to form with the cavalry, and advance, in order to sustain the infantry, which he thought to be then engaged. Colonel Sloper deposed that Captain Wintzingerode, upon Lord George's appearing not to understand the orders he delivered in French, pronounced them as well as he could in English, expressing that the movement was to be *to the left*, and *through the trees*, both by waving his hand, and by words.

Colonel Sloper also deposed, that it was at least a quarter of an hour after Wintzingerode left Lord George before Colonel Ligonier arrived. Colonel Ligonier deposed, that he also mentioned *moving to the left*; and Colonel Sloper confirms his evidence in this particular. It is also proved by several witnesses, that Colonel Ligonier, though he acknowledged his order differed from that of Colonel Fitzroy in number, yet insisted it was the same in *destination*, which it could not have been, if he also had not directed the movement *to the left*. Colonel Sloper also deposed that Lord George appeared *confused*, he remarked it, and said to Colonel Ligonier, 'For God's sake repeat your orders to that man, that he may not pretend not to understand them, but you see the condition he is in', this is also confirmed by the concurrent testimony of Colonel Ligonier.

Lord George to invalidate this testimony produced several witnesses, who deposed, that they heard no directions given, either by Captain Wintzingerode or Colonel Ligonier, to *move to the left*, or *through the trees*; and that they saw nothing in Lord George's manner or countenance different from what they saw at other times. To support Colonel Sloper's evidence, several witnesses were ready to depose that they *also remarked Lord George's confusion to be very great*; but Lord George earnestly insisting on their not being examined, upon a supposition that it would be producing new matter against him, under colour of a reply, they were not examined. It appears, however, from Colonel Ligonier's evidence, to whom Colonel Sloper remarked Lord George's confusion, that *he saw it,* for when Colonel Sloper said, 'you see the condition he is in', he answered '*yes*'.

Thus much as to facts; it is to be observed, that when the witnesses were asked questions of opinion arising from facts, they declined to answer them; but, if their opinion would have been favourable to Lord George, it seems unjust not to have declared it, because to decline the declaration of their opinion was to imply that it was against him; a strong presumption therefore arises that their opinion was against him; for, they cannot be supposed to have withheld any benefit that was his due, as an opinion in his favour, after it had been once asked, seems to have been.

According to the *London Gazette* of April 26th, 1760, the sentence pronounced upon Lord George Sackville was in these words:—

> This court, upon due consideration of the whole matter before them, is of opinion, that Lord George Sackville is guilty of having disobeyed the orders of Prince Ferdinand of Brunswick, whom he was, by his commission and instructions, directed to obey, as commander-in-chief, according to the rules of war; and it is the further opinion of this court, that Lord George Sackville is, and he is hereby adjudged, unfit to serve His Majesty in any military capacity whatever.

The *Gazette* adds:

> Which sentence His Majesty has been pleased to confirm. It is His Majesty's pleasure that the above sentence be given out in public orders, that officers, being convinced that neither high birth or great employments can shelter offences of such a nature, and that, feeling they are subject to censures much worse than death to a man who has any sense of honour, they may avoid the fatal consequences arising from disobedience of orders.

A further addition in the *Gazette* states:

> At the Court of St. James's, the 2oth of April, 1760: this day His Majesty in Council called for the Council Book, and ordered the name of Lord George Sackville to be struck out of the list of Privy Councillors.

The defence was weak and futile. The rejection of orders when before an enemy, because an action is daily expected, is the shallowest possible reason why the orders should not be obeyed. The Battle of Minden was not a surprise, and the orders of Ferdinand alone prove the hollowness of such a contention. Any hesitation or delay on the morning of August 1st was caused by the failure of a German general of division to send to Ferdinand the intelligence that the French were in motion. On July 30th and 31st, Ferdinand had enjoined upon general-officers to make themselves acquainted with the ground in their immediate vicinity, and particularly with the roads and paths leading to the plain. By his statement of defence, Lord George had not done so, or there could not have been so much quibbling with staff-officers about advancing, about moving to the left, or about going through the trees. The general commanding the British cavalry ought to have been out, and, his division being saddled and ready for action at one a.m., he ought not to have been in bed at six a.m.

Before a battle begins, or at a council of war, an inferior officer may expostulate with his superior, may offer advice, or may urge remonstrances, concerning the intended plan of operations. But, in the hour of action, it is his duty to obey orders, without expostulation or remonstrance. The moment of success may be lost in dispute. The chief commander is responsible for the propriety of his orders; the subordinate officers are accountable only for their obedience. A certain general at Dettingen was styled "the King's Confectioner", from his caution in preserving His Majesty's troops. Among the Romans it was death to fight without the general's orders, and the punishment may well have been greater for disobeying orders to fight.

George the Second, however, appreciated bravery. On one occasion, the judgment passed by a court-martial on two officers was put before him for signature. One officer had disobeyed the orders of his commander, and, fighting instead of retreating, he had upset his plans. The king refused to sign the order, saying, "one face the enemy and fight, he right; the other turn his back and not fight, he wrong". As an observation upon this broken English, it may be remarked that George the First was ignorant of the language.

On that account, he abstained from attending meetings of the Cabinet, although down to the end of the seventeenth century, it had been the custom for the sovereign to preside over, and take part in the deliberations of, Cabinet Councils; and, George the Second followed the example of his father. But, George the Second, when he opened his first Parliament on November 18th, 1760, was able to give great satisfaction by the statement in his speech that, "born and educated in this country, I glory in the name of Briton."

There are several significant omissions in the statement of Lord

George Sackville. He mentions the names of all those who gave evidence against him, but not a name of those who were for him, nor even an indication of them. He makes no allusion to the fact that he would not allow Lord Granby to move, nor does he mention him, his second-in-command, in support of his defence. Notwithstanding all the orders given to him, he did nothing, and, on August 1st, the cavalry did not engage the French. The order confining the action, or intended movement, to British cavalry was sent by Ferdinand, when he found Sackville did not obey his first orders, because he thought that it was safeguarding British susceptibilities.

✶✶✶✶✶✶

In the Annual Register for 1760, on page 178, immediately following the sentence on Lord George Sackville, are the particulars relating to the interment of King George the Second.

✶✶✶✶✶✶

In the Annual Register for 1760, on page 241, there is an epigram on the Marquis of Granby, who was born bald, and there is also an ode on his losing his hat and charging the French lines bareheaded. From the former is the following extract:—

> *Caesar was prematurely bare,*
> *just as is honour'd Rutland's heir,*
> *and, to conceal his want of hair,*
> *contrived the laurel-wreath to wear.*
>
> . . . . . . .
> *Hold . . . . . ,*
> *. . . . Granby too his bareness pains,*
> *and, therefore, in Westphalia's plains,*
> *he vindicates the British quarrel,*
> *and wreathes about his brows the laurel.*

**GENERAL MAP OF THE SCENE of OPERATIONS**

Uchte
Stolzenau
Neustadt
Gr. Burgwedel
Rehburg
Steinhuder Meer
Steinhude
Bohnhorst
Wunstorf
Sachsenhagen
Petershagen
Leine
Linden
Hannover
Minden
Weser
Stadthagen
Rodenberg
Dohren
Apelern
Bückeburg
Bücke B.
Deister G.
Wennigsen
Pattensen
Weser
Oeynhausen
Rinteln
Vlotho
Geb.
Munder
Springe
Innerste
Varenholz
Oldendorf
Eldagsen
Hohenhausen
Exten
Koppenbrügge
Hildesheim
Hameln
Elze
Bosingfeld
Lauenstein
Gronau
Lemgo
Aerzen
Salzhemmendorf
Brake
Alverdissen
Lage
Grohnde
Saale
Pyrmont
Duingen
Werre
Detmold
Blomberg
Lugde
Ottenstein
Afeld
Emmer
Delligsen
Polle
Eschershausen
Schwalenberg
Horn
Steinheim
Stadtoldendorf
Lippe
Altaxen
Holzminden
Nieheim
Einbeck
Lippspringe
Dassel
Salzderhelden
Hoxter
Egge
Leine
Driburg
Weser
Sollinger Wald
Ilme
Brakel
Nethe
Northeim
Dringenberg
Moringen
Beverungen
Lichtenau
Willebadessen
Uslar
Karlshafen
Hardegsen
Nethe
Borgholz
G.
Helmarshausen
Bodenfelde
Sauer
Borgentreich
Gottsbüren
Bovenden
Sielen
Reinhards
Adelebsen
Diemel
Göttingen
Warburg
hards
Veckerhagen
Nd. Marsberg
Liebenau
Hofgeismar
Dransfeld
Wald
Reinhausen
Volkmarsen
Arolsen
Münden
Wilhelmsthal
Fulda
Mengeringhausen
Werra
Hedemünden
Zierenberg
Wolfhagen
Cassel
Witzenhausen

# Vellinghausen
By Charles Townshend

February l7th, 1761. Major-General Townshend set out for the army in Germany.

Such was the notice in the *Gentleman's Magazine*. He had had about a year's leave after returning from Quebec, and was now given command of the 2nd Brigade in the field force in Germany under the Marquess of Granby, who commanded the British contingent sent to aid the army of Prince Ferdinand of Brunswick, fighting now against the French in Westphalia.

Considerable reinforcements of the line had left England for Germany in the spring of 1760, and the second battalions of the Foot Guards (3,000) were sent in July, embarking at Gravesend. The total British force under the Marquess of Granby on the field state was 32,000 combatants.

The composition of the army corps was as follows:—

LIEUT.-GENERAL THE HONBLE. HENRY CONWAY'S CORPS.

Infantry
- 1st *Brigade* (Brigadier-General Cæsar).
  - Grenadiers of the Foot Guards.
  - 2nd battalion 1st Foot Guards.
  - „     „     Coldstream Guards.
  - „     „     3rd Foot Guards.

Infantry
- 2nd *Brigade* (Brigadier-General the Honble. George Townshend).
  - 8th, King's (Barrington's).
  - 25th Foot.
  - 50th  „   (Carr's).
  - 20th  „   (Kingsley's).

Cavalry *Brigade* (Brigadier-General Douglas).
- 1st Dragoons (Bland's), 3 squadrons.
- Howard's Dragoons, 2 squadrons.
- 5th Dragoon Guards (Waldegrave's), 2 squadrons.

LIEUT.-GENERAL MARQUESS OF GRANBY'S CORPS.

Infantry
- 1st Brigade (Brigadier-General Beckwith).
  - Waldegrave's Foot.
  - Maxwell's "
  - Campbell's "
  - Keith's "
- 2nd Brigade (Brigadier-General Waldegrave).
  - 5th Foot (Hodgson's).
  - 24th " (Cornwallis's).
  - 37th " (Stuart's).
  - 12th " (Napier's).

Cavalry Brigade.
- Scots Greys, 2 squadrons.
- 11th Light Dragoons (Ancrum's), 2 squadrons.
- 7th " " (Mostyn's), 2 squadrons.

Besides Artillery.

When Townshend reached the army, it was in winter quarters, his own brigade being at Paderborn with Conway's corps. It is interesting to note that Gerard Lake, who was afterwards to win fame as Lord Lake of Laswaree, was present, serving his first campaign as a subaltern in the Grenadier Guards in General Caesar's brigade of Guards.

All the four battalions in Townshend's brigade were distinguished regiments,—the famous 20th (the East Devon), then known as Kingsley's Regiment, changed in the present day to the Lancashire Fusiliers; its name had been made by Wolfe, who commanded it after Culloden, and the regiment had made itself famous at the Battle of Minden, in the same country where Townshend was now campaigning, two years before; it was in the 20th (then Bligh's) that Townshend had got his company after Fontenoy; since those days the 20th has always maintained its glorious reputation: the 50th (Carr's), destined to make a great name in the Peninsula in Rowland Hill's division: the 8th or King's, which began to be famous with Blenheim: and the 25th King's Own Scottish Borderers, a regiment which has ever been second to none. Townshend wrote in a letter:

> I think myself happy in having Corps and Field officers of such reputation, in this Brigade.

It was indeed a brigade to be proud of.

In the earlier part of the campaign in 1760 Prince Ferdinand of Brunswick had held the French in check, who, under the command of the Duc de Broglie and Soubise, had tried to penetrate into Hanover. Prince Ferdinand had especially handled them severely at Warburg on July 31st, 1760, where the French had lost 1,500 men and ten guns. (Referred to in the "Letter to an Honble. Brigadier" after

Quebec). The British troops had upheld their good name, and were always placed in the post of honour; consequently they suffered very severe losses, but in return were invariably lavishly praised by Prince Ferdinand in his dispatches.

The French were in possession of Cassel and Gottingen. In March the allied army advanced, the French retiring before them to Hesse-Cassel; 7,000 Prussians reinforced the Allied Army, and the enemy were driven from Langensalza. The French retired to Fulda, and then to Frankfort-on-Main, their magazines established about the country being nearly all destroyed. Prince Ferdinand then laid siege to Cassel with the German troops, whilst the British force was posted as a corps of observation. Townshend's brigade was detached from the main body, as I gather from the following letters of his, dated in May from Soist, Weidenbruck, and Hamm.

I quote these in full, as they are of interest to a soldier, giving some idea of the training of our officers in those days. It will be seen that Townshend is always asking for entrenching tools (in the present day entrenching tools have become of equal importance with ammunition). In the way of military precautions our force in Germany in 1761 was certainly as far advanced as the arrangements of today (I speak with regard to reconnaissance, outposts, advanced and rear guards, etc.), perhaps even more so, when one reflects on the number of times our troops have been taken by surprise in the latest campaign. Ferdinand of Brunswick, it must be remembered, was an apt pupil and lieutenant of Frederick the Great, who held always that it was pardonable for an officer to be defeated, but that there is no pardon for the officer who is surprised.

To Lt. General Conway at Soist (par Estafette).

Weidenbruck 23 May 1761.

I had the honour of receiving your commands dated 21 May, and those of the 22nd, last night by Estafette. I am sorry I could not send you the report of the brigade sooner. I waited for that from the Kings Regiment (which was sent to Soist by mistake) as soon as I received it, I forwarded the whole returns with all expedition. I should be very unhappy if in this or any other article the execution of your orders in this brigade appeared to be dilatory or neglected, for I can assure you Sir, no one is more ambitious of executing to your satisfaction than myself. I observe by your orders of the 21st that I am directed to report

A Soldier of Townshend's Regiment (the 28th)

what forage I find in this neighbourhood and endeavour to form what depot or magazines I can for the troops under my command, and to take care the deliverys are regular and according to the effective horses.

Upon my arrival here I found a Jew who had forage, he had furnisht the 24th at this place, I accordingly foraged the whole Brigade from him until further orders. He applied to me for an order to demand horses from the magistrates to bring up more. Upon reading your orders, and having then none to forage elsewhere I thought myself authorised to give such orders upon the country, he first shewing me authority from Colonel Peirson to establish magazines.

Be pleased to favour me with your directions whether I am to continue this order to this Jew, or withdraw it? whether I am to order the brigade to continue to forage here, or to forage at the places as directed in your last order of the 22. I have reconnoitred some of the roads and communications of the cantonments, they are very bad and almost impracticable since these rains. I shall take care that the commanding officers of the brigade inform themselves minutely concerning them, and you shall very soon have an exact description of the state and distances of the whole.

As I was out reconnoitring the roads the greatest part of yesterday, I have not yet been able to fix upon the signals, but I shall do that immediately and report them to you. Have you any particular directions to give me for the conduct of my brigade in case of any alarm or emergency? am I to give such orders as may appear to me the most proper upon a view of their position. I was at Stromberg yesterday, it is 2 leagues from hence to the S. P. the roads impracticable to artillery and baggage; it is situated upon a considerable height, it is so woody that they can see no signal I make from hence; it is an open village. 3 companys of the Kings are there.

It is 2 stone from Waterloo the other quarters, very bad roads and 2½ stone from Leisborne. The roads forwards to Hamm are bad. Buken is the next town towards Hamm is 2½ leagues from Stromberg. Hamm is 4½ leagues from thence. I am going round the other cantonments to day. I should have been glad to have saved you the trouble of reading this long letter by waiting on you, but that I remain here to execute your orders concerning the discipline and economy of the several regiments be punctually executed. I think myself happy in having corps and field officers of such reputation, in this brigade.

Some of them complain to me that their Independant draughts (not reviewed I believe by Lord Frederick Cavendish) are unfit for service. Would you please I should look them over and report them? Carr's, (50th Regiment), has 2 waggon loads of stores they dont want; what do you please to order I should do with such stores as only embarrass the regiments, and where would you have them sent. Where are we to send for Pioneers implements. We can gett none here.

    I have the honour to be etc.

                 Geo. Townshend.

P.S.: The men quartered in this town have good rooms; it has an old rampart round it, but no parapet, a ditch fordable in several places, 4 gates with draw bridges. I have ordered post guards, and the brigades to be drawn up at retreat beating. It is the best post the companys at Stromberg could fall back upon in case of an alarm as it is as near as any of their own quarters. This is 2 stone from Retburg. The roads between these two last places not so bad as they are forwards. I beg leave to enclose a letter about a deserter from Major Boisragon. There are 2 companys of Independants just arrived here. I shall divide them and send them off to the regiments. I'm sorry to send so foul a letter, but write in very great haste.

  From Majr. Genl. Townshend to Lt. Genl. Howard.

             Weidenbruck 24 May 1761.

Dear Sir

I am very sorry that the returns of the brigade should not give satisfaction. I have ordered them to be explained by the commanding officers of the several regiments with all possible dispatch, and you and General Conway will I hope be so good as to consider, that as I am so lately appointed to this brigade, they were the first returns that ever came to my hands, and consequently that the great difference between these and the preceding could not strike me; this I only begg leave to observe in excuse, for what may appear otherwise great inattention on my part; give me leave to assure you on this occasion that I am too well convinced how essential it is for everyone to be active on his station, for to desire to give my superiors any unnecessary trouble; the very distant situation of some of the quarters of this cantonment and the extreme bad and inundated state of the roads has prevented (I believe) in a great measure the speedy execution of orders.

When the orders come here they pass through quarters to which they must return from thence answers and reports must come back here, before we send a more general report; however be assured that every method will be taken to expedite every order and service commanded.

The orderly officer was sent as my major of brigade assures me without loss of time and such was the state of roads that he was obliged to swim his horse thrice, and I was much in the same situation on reconnoitring the country according to Genl. Conway's orders of which I send him a description as far as I had gone. Please to tell him that tomorrow morning I will reconnoitre as far as Hamm myself. I was yesterday evening at Langenbrück, the roads are very indifferent, and if I have not Pioneers tools, I fear on a forced march any way we must leave our baggage and perhaps artillery behind. The inclosed report of the artillery offrs. (left by mistake yesterday on my table) increases my apprehensions on this article.

If I had pioneers tools I am sure I could do a great deal. There might be very good roads made here every way, by new roads and now and then felling a few willow trees, and laying them over with fascines; where otherwise in the present roads, baggage and cannon will be all laid fast—and I would observe moreover that the Boors have ditched up all the old march routes, which are good and might be restored in a few minutes, if we had proper instruments.

I have not yet got the return of the officers of the brigade capable to serve as Engineers or of artificers. I hope to send you that, this evening or tomorrow forenoon, and an exact account of the country towards Hamm. I expect the offrs. of the different regiments are all this day reconnoitring the country communicating to their several cantonments and further as directed by Genl. Conway's letter.

The Independants, arrived here, were 185, they were divided for the oldest brigades 62 to the 3rd 61, they were seven deserters sent this day to Soist and five not taken, drawn for by the 12

GEORGE TOWNSHEND.

battns. of infantry, I gave the offrs. commanding them proper march routes one to Soist through Lepstadt, the other to turn off from thence to Erwille with orders to halt discretionarly as they found quarters.

I do not recollect anything Sir that I have omitted mentioning to you that has not be said to Genl. Conway sooner if I had been desirous of reporting the Independant Companys then arriving.

     I have the honour to be
      Dr. Sir etc.
              Geo. Townshend.
    To Lts General Conway.
            Ham, 26th May, 1761.

Dear Sir,

I have taken the first opportunity to endeavour to send you a description of this part of the country, according to your orders, by an Estafette which Major Stockhausen is sending to you; it is in my power to transmit an immediate (tho imperfect account) of what I have reconnoitred. The roads from Weidenbruck to Stromberg are much mended within these few days, yet require assistance; the distance from thence to Beckham is three leagues, the roads better, after one league good marching in general by subdivisions; there is a commanding height called Mackenberg on the left, a good post, from whence you command the country to the N.W. and the course of the Lippe to the west lower than Ham.

The country round Beckham is more open, and the roads pretty good to the Lippe, where is a good post, at a *chateau* called Hourcharen a league and one half from Ham. Here is a bridge over the Lippe and two other *chateaux*.

The meadows are wide and the commanding heights are at a considerable distance from the river, that height called Heiungberg is the most commanding. The bottom from this to the *chateau* before mentioned is bad and from thence to this place is a league and a half, the roads sandy tho good.

The fortifications very contemptible, you will excuse my not being more particular a great way to get home, I must go some part of it this night, when I receive the general report of the brigade tomorrow, I shall draw out the best state I can of the roads, the distances and calculations necessary for marching. In the interim, I flatter myself you will be pleased to accept of this imperfect state of it, as a proof of my desires to obey your commands on all occasions.

        I am, Dear Sir,
            Yours, etc.,
                  Geo. Townshend.

                Weidenbruck, May 30th 1761.

Dear Sir,

I have the honour of transmitting to you a report of the brigade under my command as cantoned, with the distances of the several quarters from hence, their bearings from the church of this place and some observations on the posts. I remained the night of the 26th at Ham that I might have an opportunity of making some remarks next day on the country to the right of the Lippe, nearer the river than that part described in my letter from Ham. The distance from that place to Dabourg is a league and one half; the roads good; from thence to Nutrop a league and from thence to Lippebourg one league and a half, the roads practicable for carriages.

There is a ford near Lippebourg which is passable for men and horses, when the river is not swelled by the falling rains. The distance from Lippebourg to Hersfield is two leagues, the roads good for one English mile and the rest very bad and heavy, the village open, there is a castle called Hofstadt opposite to it.

From Hersfield to Leisburn the distance is two leagues the roads pretty good, but as this last mentioned place is one of our quarters described in the report, I shall not now trouble you on that subject. The country in general is strong and much wood in it, and such (in my judgment) that cavalry should have difficulty to act in. The Lippe is fordable in many places from Ham to Lippestadt. Want of time has prevented my reconnoitring any part of the country on the left of the Lippe as directed by your letter. If that is thought necessary I shall take the first opportunity of doing it, as I shall at all times be ready to execute your orders according to the best of my abilities.

I forward reports and returns with all the expedition of the situation of the several quarters can admit of, and if unforseen accidents occasion any delay, I hope the adj. genl. shall take the trouble to write to my major of brigade before mention is made of it in public orders, I shall give further directions about sending immediately these returns called for by the order of the 24th.

    I am, Sir, etc.,

                Geo. Townshend.

Early in the month of July, 1761, Prince Ferdinand of Brunswick, obliged to raise the siege of Cassel, had taken position behind the Salzbach, with his left wing resting on the south bank of the Lippe, to the east of Hamm, near the small villages of Vellinghausen and Hohenover, and he there determined to await the attack of De Broglie and Soubise, who had formed a junction in the same month. The French numbered about 160,000 combatants, against Prince Ferdinand's 95,000; but, happily for the allies, De Broglie and Soubise were jealous of one another, with the usual friction and misunderstandings common in an army among generals of equal rank.

I quote several orders from George Townshend's order-book of the 2nd Brigade, as they give a very clear idea of what the discipline and training in the army were like in those days. These orders show that all military precautions were taken as regards advanced guards, outposts, etc., that the expenditure of ammunition in action was properly controlled, and that the baggage arrangements were excellent. When in touch with the enemy, the army had to be dressed and ready to march at 3 am. I have *The Regulations for the Prussian Infantry by Frederick the Great* which belonged to the old *marquess*, and I find that everything in this campaign was carried out according to the regulations of that great soldier; they are excellent, and very little improved on today.

When in touch with the enemy, every soldier had to have sixty rounds in his pouches; this was a standing order. It is true the orders are somewhat long and repeat themselves, but I am not sure that they are the worse for that, and I feel certain that they will be of interest to military readers. The order-book I have of this campaign is entitled "*Orderly Book of the 2nd Brigade of British Infantry, under the orders of Major General The Honourable George Townshend,*" dating from June 26th, 1761, Soist, to November 2nd, 1761. (This order-book is kept in the handwriting of a non-commissioned officer, and many of the names of persons and places are spelt wrong.—C.V. F.T.)

With the exception of the few letters I publish of George Townshend's in this campaign, I have not got a single letter to write from, so I draw largely on the order-book. I cannot find any private letters of Townshend's relating to this campaign, except those written to his wife, which are not of a nature interesting to readers of military history.

"CAMP AT SOIST 27*th June* 1761.
" *Parole* . . .
" *Countersign* . . .
For the day to-morrow Lieut: Genl. Conway

| | | | |
|---|---|---|---|
| *Major Generals* | Cavalry | . . | Col. Gold |
| | Infantry | . . | Lord Pembroke |
| *Picquets this night* | British Guards | . . | Lt. Col. Clark |
| | British Infantry | . . | Lt. Col. Dallop |
| | Hanoverian | . . | Major Hallnel |
| | Brunswick | . . | Major Hardwick |
| | Hesse | . . | Lt. Col. Harwine |
| | Cavalry | . . | Lieut. Col. Last |
| *Majors of Brigade* | Webber | | |
| | Courtenay | | |

The Army is hereby ordered to remain assembled together and every soldier to keep in camp. Those regiments that are in want of forage must endeavour to procure it as near camp as possible. At 6 in the evening the army will strike their tents and pack up the baggage and the regiments shall form up on their parades, the infantry will ground their arms and stay by them; the cavalry to remain with their horses.

As soon as the regiments are formed on their parades, each soldier is to be served with 60 cartridges of ammunition; the wagons may be left behind.

The following officers are appointed to assist Lieut. Col. Pitt in the superintendence of Forage-Infantry Lt. Col. Rolt 11 Regt.; Quartermaster Hardy of ditto. Cavalry Major Sandford Carabiniers. Captain Whitmore Inniskillings. Lieut. Walker of B lands; Lieutenant Abercrombie of Howard's; the assistant Quartermasters are also to be under Lieut. Col. Pitt's orders on this Duty.

*After Orders 4 o'clock.*

H.S.H. the Duke orders that the picquets of the army both cavalry and infantry are to assemble precisely at 4 o'clock this afternoon in the front of the 3rd regiment of British Guards together with the field officers of the picquets; likewise the generals of the day will assemble at the same place, from whom the field officers of the picquet will receive orders for their destination. Four light 6 pounders to be furnished from the British Park of Artillery to be at the same rendezvous.

The order given this morning for the tents to be struck at 6 o'clock this evening is countermanded and they are not to be struck till further orders.

*After Orders 7 at night.*

The regimts. to send to Mr. Rheden at Soist to know how many days bread he can supply them with, to make up 8 days bread with that they have already with them, they are to receive as much as will complete them for 8 days, if there is sufficient, and report directly to the major of brigade to what time they are supplied.

The regimts. Likewise are to report if they have made up cartridges to complete to 60 rounds per man, and what number they have made besides to furnish the complement wanting for their respective Tumbrils.

*After Orders half past 8 at night.*

The disposition of the march of the army from the camp at Soist, the army will march by the left in 6 collumns by subdivisions exactly at 12 oclock this night, 6 collumns Coldstreams Regime, at the head 3rd Regimt., first Regimt. Grenadiers of the Guards, Griffins, Bocklands, Waldegraves, Howards, Blands, Lieut. Genl. Conway will command this collumn.

Each under the orders of a field officer will form the advance guard respectively; the collumns will march well closed and no carriages no batt. horses to be suffered within the collumns excepting the field pieces and ammunition waggon to each cannon, the batt. horses are to follow their collumns according to the order of march; after them, the other ammunition waggons, then the chaise of bread waggons, the chaplain and surgeons waggon, and lastly the sutlers waggon, the whole in order of march in their respective regiments.

Every genl. officer leading a collumn will appoint an officer to regulate the march of the baggage. The baggage belonging to Lord Granby's Corps will remain upon the present ground till the first collumn have past by it, when it will fall in the rear.

The officers to be particularly attentive to their platoons and divisions.

A regimental court martial to be held after coming to the ground in each regimt., to try and punish on the spot all such men as shall, unnecessarily stay behind on the march.

The baggage and carriages of the 6 collumns the (*vizt.*) the infirmary and bread waggons and batt horses are all to remain in the rear of the camp of their respective regiments till the troops of the whole collumn are past, as soon as Blands Regiment of Dragoon Guards are past, the Baggage of the General officers the (*vizt.*) Lieut. Genl. Conway, Major Genl. Caesar Lord Frederick Cavendish and Major Genl. Douglass to follow that regiment then the baggage of Coldstream Regt. of Guards followed by that of the other regiments of this column in the same order the regimts. marched after Coldstream the 3rd Regimt. of Guards, then first Grenadiers, Griffins, Bocklands, Waldegraves, Howards and Blands, any driver or conductor breaking into this order, will be punished on the spot.

"H.S.H. orders that half after 11 o'clock a cannon shall be fired which is to serve as a signal for the tents to be struck and for the whole army to form in order of battle, a second cannon that will be fired at 12 upon which the army will march off according to the disposition above given at the signal of the first cannon that the picquets of each collumn will assemble at the head of their respective collumns, the empty bread waggons to be left behind at the bakery at Soist, to bring up bread for their respective regts.

A subaltern per brigade to put the baggage in march according to the above order, who is then to join the regiment.

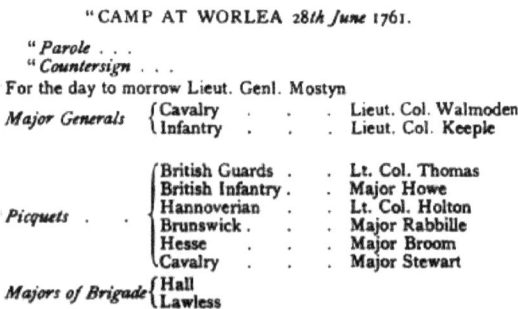

The soldiers are not to absent themselves from or quit the camp and are to hold themselves in constant readiness to march.

The regiments to forrage tomorrow morning according to the disposition of the order which will be given out to them for that purpose by Lieut. Col. Pitt.

The regiments are to provide themselves with bread to the 4th July inclusive, and for the future they must endeavour to keep bread up to the same time, when they send for it to Lippstadt they are to pass the Lippe at Overstadt, and are not to go through Soust, the Guards to continue making up cartridges till the ammunition is compleated.

When the regiments want wood it is to be a standing order that no man is to be suffered to go out for it without officers to attend them.

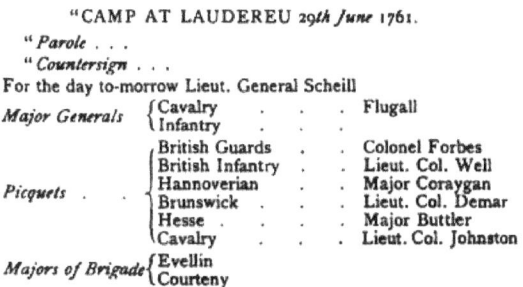

The new picquet of the whole infantry, will march immediately, the British and Hessian will be assembled at the head of the Hessian Infy. of the first line, the Brunswicks and Hannoverians at the head of the Hannoverian guards, Lieut. Col. Keppel has already reed. H.S.H. orders and instructions for posting them.

As soon as the said picquet of the collumns of this morning will rejoin their regiments.

At one o'clock tomorrow morning the whole camp to be dresst and accoutered the cavalry saddled and the artillery park as well as the regiments field pieces to be harnest.

All the empty bread waggons to be sent immediately to Lippstadt for bread, a subaltern officer to be appointed to attend them, who is to be as expeditious as possible to bring them back.

*Morning Orders the 30th June 1761.*

The cavalry may unsaddle and the men be at liberty to go on with the usual camp business, but no man must be suffered to straggle from camp, and the whole to be kept in readiness to march at the shortest notice.

The British to forrage immediately as near the camp as possible, the forragers of the infantry will assemble in the rear of the brigade of Guards the whole will receive their instructions from Lieut. Colonel Pitt.

"CAMP AT KAMALAU 5th July 1761.

"*Parole* . . .
"*Countersign* . . .
For the day to morrow Lieut. Genl. Howard

| Major Generals | Cavalry . . . . | Col. Walden |
| --- | --- | --- |
| | Infantry . . . | Genl. Townshend |
| Picquets . . | British Guards . | Lt. Col. Steele |
| | „ Line . . | Lt. Col. Wells |
| | Hannoverian . . | Major Hardenburg |
| | Brunswick . . | Major Wardorph |
| | Hesse . . . | Major Black |
| | Cavalry . . | Major Kelliott |
| Majors of Brigade | Hall | |
| | Courteny | |

The collumns may return to their former ground from which they marched this morning and the new Infantry Picquets will march immediately with one field piece per battalion, and be posted in the front of the camp. The major genls. of the day for the infantry will see they are properly posted.

The New Grand Guard to be posted immediately and the cavy. picquets are to march at 8 this evening. The major genl. of the day of the cavalry will post them so as to sustain the infantry picquets.

The park of artillery are to return to the encampment they occupied last night.

"CAMP AT HOHENOVER 15th July 1761.

"*Parole* . . .
"*Countersign* . . .
For the day to morrow Lieut. Gen. Conway.

| Major Generals | Cavalry . . . . | Ohaiml |
| --- | --- | --- |
| | Infantry . . . | Boke |
| Picquets . . | British Guards . | Lt. Col. Scott |
| | Line . . . | Lt. Col. Graham |

As long as the army remains in this position a field officer is to be ordered for the picquets of each of the four divisions, of which it is composed. The commanding officers of each division, are to order one cavalry captain for the picquets of the cavalry attached to it, with the usual number of men and squadron in the village of Illingzenand the house Late General Conway's quarters.

H.S.H. ordered to be posted yesterday in the afternoon a captain and a 100 men from the Prince of Anhalt's division with orders to keep up a communication with Genl. Howard's Division upon his right and the Prince of Anhalt's division upon his left, as also to push his posts forwards, in order to gain the earliest intelligence of any movements of the enemy towards them.

This detachment to be relieved at 5 this afternoon by Lieut. Genl. Howard's division.

One captain and 100 infantry from the Prince of Anhalt's division is posted at the bridge of Curtamuhl which is also to be relieved at 5 this afternoon, by the same division, a captain and 100 infantry to be posted likewise at 5 this afternoon at the Nawmuhl, which are to be furnished by Lieut GenL Watgenaw's division, which division has also posted an officer and 40 at the chateau called Madenau, and an officer and 50 at the Schwainmuhl. All these posts during the army continuance in its present position are to be relieved every 24 hours, that the men may be kept more alert whilst on duty,

H.S.H. orders that every officer who is posted with a detachment in any redoubt fleches or other fortified posts is to maintain and defend himself in it to the utmost, and not to abandon or retire from it, till he sees there is no possibility of keeping it any longer or that he receives orders to quit it from his superior officers, and in that case he is to make his retreat in good order, and with the best countenance, this being the only means to prevent the enemys pursuing him otherwise than with great precaution. Every retreat that is made in a hurry and in confusion will easily be overpowered and entirely demolished there being nothing to stop the enemy. Every officer is to make it an essential point of his duty to preserve upon all such occasions a good countenance and to exhort his troops to the same as his own honour that of his command and the common safety of both depends upon it.

As these detachments are equally posted at no great distance from camp, every general officer of the day, or other genls. of the army who may happen to be at hand and receive the first accounts of any posts being attacked, he is go there immediately, without waiting or sending for orders from the headquarters, and order up some picquets and even some pieces of cannon to sustain the post, sending only an immediate report by an officer to H.S.H. if any regiments ground have been spoiled by the rain. H.S.H. allows it to look out for better in its rear.

*After orders past 7 in the evening.*

The baggage and carriages to be loaded, and ready to march off on the first order. The whole to be kept assembled in camp and ready to turn out upon the shortest notice.

## The Battle of Vellinghausen, or Kirch Deukern

De Broglie and Soubise had joined hands at Soist, and determined to attack Prince Ferdinand in his position south of the Lippe, between Hamm and Lippstadt; for the allies were actually between them and the Rhine. Prince Ferdinand soon heard of their intentions, and took up a strong position. The River Aest runs a considerable way almost parallel to the Lippe, from which it is not distant in some places more than half a mile. The high road from Lippstadt to Hamm passes between these rivers, and it was of the greatest importance to Ferdinand to secure that important communication, for it was his only advantageous line of retreat, by which he could still retain a command over the adjacent country.

With a view, therefore, of protecting that communication, he established his left wing on the isthmus between the two rivers. The left extremity of that wing stretched as far north as the Lippe, by which it was perfectly secured, as the right flank of that wing was supported by the village of Kirch Deukern, on the River Aest.

At the village of Kirch Deukern another river, called the Salzbach, small but very deep, joins the Aest almost at a right angle.

Behind this river (*i.e.* west of the Salzbach), on a considerable eminence, was placed the centre, under Lieut.-General Conway, and on a continuation of this eminence the right wing, under the Hereditary Prince, stretched south towards the village of Werle, its flank being well secured by the rugged, bushy, and impracticable ground.

Thus, Ferdinand of Brunswick had a river in front of his centre and right wing, and the left wing was supported by rivers on both flanks.

Prince Ferdinand considered that the French would attack his left wing, and so he placed the bulk of his artillery there; and he was right.

On July 15th, at six in the evening, Lord Granby's advanced posts were attacked with the greatest fury by the French. His division, formed of the Guards Brigade and Townshend's brigade, maintained its ground manfully, defending the village of Vellinghausen by a house-to-house defence—as Prince Ferdinand described it, with "*unbeschreiblicher Tapferkeit.*" Their task was a hard one, for the French showed all their wonted élan in the attack. At last Wutgenau, with his Hanoverians, on the extreme left, reinforced Granby, and the French were repulsed after four hours' desperate fighting, falling back into the woods. Firing ceased at 10 p.m.

During the night, Prince Ferdinand shifted the British troops to behind the Salzbach (see sketch), Wutgenaus Hanoverians being told

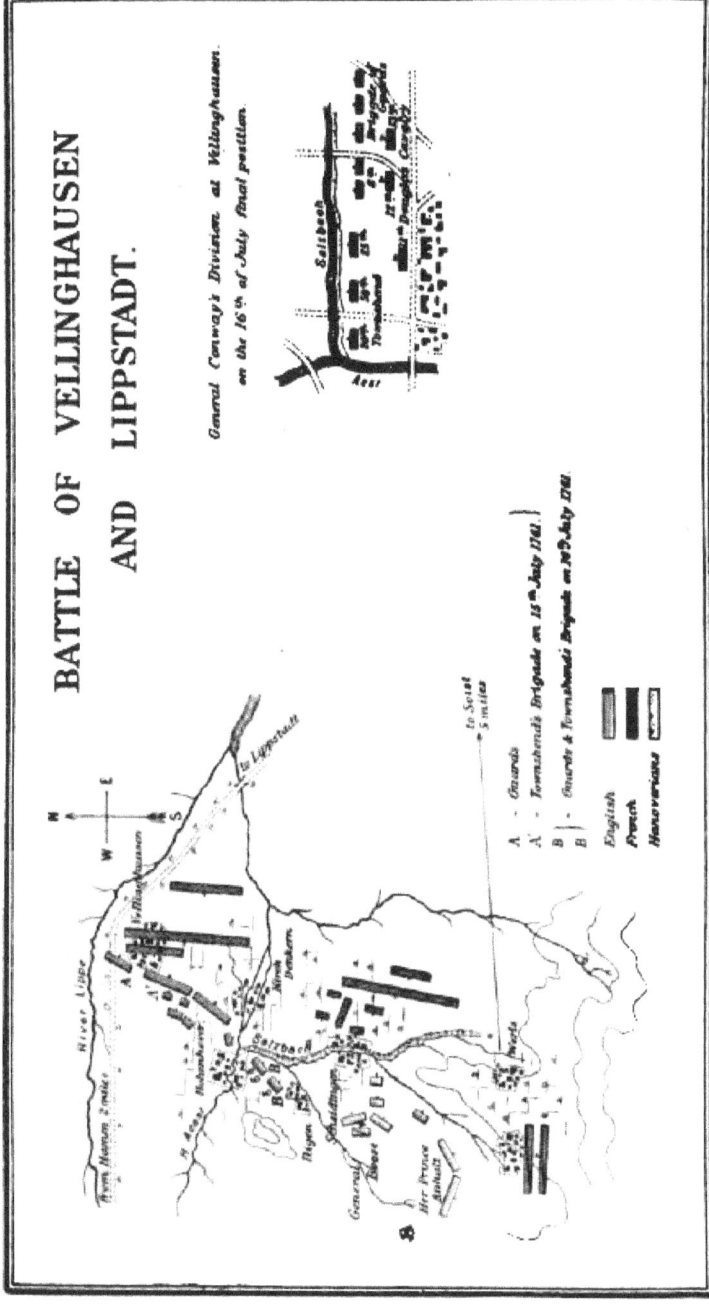

off to hold Vellinghausen. At 3 a.m. the French attacked again, De Broglie commanding in person; and again, Vellinghausen was their main objective. Prince Soubise commanded the French centre and left. For five hours, the action raged, the Hanoverians under Wutgenau bearing the brunt and rivalling the conduct of the British.

At 9 a.m. Prince Ferdinand saw that the French were bringing up guns on to an eminence opposite Lord Granby's position; he at once called up his reserve under General Sporken, and, having reinforced his first line, ordered a general advance, the French retiring all along the line in disorder. Soubise, in command of the French left and centre, had not even been able to pass the Salzbach, and had simply confined his efforts to artillery fire; he promptly followed the example of the French right wing. The close nature of the country, the hollow roads, favoured the French retreat, it is true, but it should have also favoured the pursuit. However, the French were unpursued in their retirement, and so the victory was barren of results.

The allies lost 311 killed and 1,011 wounded, and 192 missing. The French loss was estimated at 5,000 killed and wounded, 9 guns, and 6 colours. The reputation of our British infantry was greatly enhanced in this battle.

"CAMP AT HOHENOVER 16th July 1761.

"*Parole* . . .
"*Countersign* . . .
For the day to morrow Lieut. Genl. Moyston
*Major Generals* {Cavalry . . . . Douglass
{Infantry . . . . Bishausen

Divine service to be performed tomorrow morning and the whole army to return thanks to Almighty God for the victory obtained this day over the enemy, a *Feu de Joie* tomorrow evening the time for which will be given out in orders, tomorrow. The regiments are to recomplet themselves this evening with cartridges for the field pieces, as well as for small arms.
A return to be given in of the killed, wounded, and missing of the picquets of the British in this day's action.

*Morning orders 17th July 1761.*

At 6 o'clock this evening, the army and all the detached corps are to be under arms, in the front of the camp to fire the *Feu de Joie*. The artillery taken from the enemy will begin it, followed by the artillery attached to each Corps; the field pieces of the regiments, lastly small arms. The whole to be repeated three times beginning upon the right of each corps.

"CAMP AT HOHENOVER 17th July 1761.

"*Parole* . . .
"*Countersign* . . .
For the day to morrow Lieut. Genl. Howard

*Major Generals* { Cavalry . . . . Elliot
                  { Infantry . . . . Harling

*Picquets* { Picquets { British Guards . Lt. Col. Clark
          {          { „ Line . Lt. Col. Prescott
          { Lieut.Genl. Howard's division  Lt. Col. Napier
          { Prince of Anhalt's . . Major Swaydorph
          { Lieut. Genl. Watgenaw's . Major Caritzdock

The post of Illingson of a captain and 100 infantry to be relieved immediately by Major Genl. Townshend's brigade. The corps of Lieut. Genl. Conway, Lieut. Genl. Howard, the Prince of Anhalt and Lieut. Genl. Watgenaw's are to order out some workmen, to cut down the hedges and underwood in the front, after which is done, the picquets are to be advanced beyond the Saltzbach, on the other side of which, they are also to cut down the wood and to make good ouvertures.

A chain to be formed of the picquets under cover of which the regiments may forrage. The field pieces of the regiments are also to be advanced near the Saltzbach. The general officers of the day and field officers of the picquets are to take care that this is done tomorrow.

A surgeon from every regiment in the army and detached corps to be sent immediately to Ham to be employed in applying the first dressings to the poor wounded which are in great numbers there.

The glorious victory of yesterday furnishes H.S.H. with a fresh opportunity to testify to the troops which he has the honour to command the highest esteem and perfect consideration he has for them on account of the good countenance which they shewed for so long a time, notwithstanding the redoubled fire of the artillery and musquetry of the enemy and afterwards by the vigorous and intrepid attack by which they overpowered and drove them from all their posts.

H.S.H. therefore, hereby makes them his most sincere and perfect acknowledgments and declares to them that as their general he has the utmost reason to be satisfied with that conduct and bravery which the generals, field officers, and others, as also the cause of the different nations have had an opportunity to shew and who have distinguished themselves by their good will and intrepidity, that it is most sensible pleasure to him to make this public declaration of it to them that he will not only remember it as long as he lives, but to retain for them a perpetual esteem and friendship and will not fail moreover to recommend them, to their respective sovereigns, that they may be by them rewarded as they so justly deserve.

H.S.H. further thinks it proper that the army should be acquainted of what passed upon the right, while our left was engaged with the enemy *vizt* that almost Marshall Soubise's whole army manoeuvred opposite the Hereditary Prince's corps endeavouring to penetrate in several places but that the Prince by his prudent manoeuvres, his own personal bravery and that of his troops rendered their attempts ineffectual so that they were obliged to retire with great loss, which contributed not a little to our being able on the left to push with our advantages with more certainty and success with regard to the two princes of Brunswick Frederick and Henry they have well supported by their behaviour yesterday that good opinion, which was with so much justice entertained of them before, having in their first campaign and at their first action they have been in, showing so much presence of mind and so good a countenance and have acted with so much intrepidity.

The eldest at the head of his own regiment and both in places of the greatest danger. H.S.H. feels a particular pleasure in declaring this himself to the army, and to make known to these two princes, his satisfaction and aprobation of them. H.S.H. also looks upon it as an essential a point from gratitude as well as friendship to make his first and most sincere acknowledgements to his Excellency the Count de Lippe for the fatiguable pains in arranging ordering and executing with such surprising expedition everything within his power towards contributing to the glorious success of the day. H.S.H. declares for himself and also in the name of common cause to preserve the most lasting remembrance of and gratitude for it.

The action of yesterday is to take the name of Vellinghausen which is to be declared to the army. Any corps which has taken trophies from the enemy is to report it to Adjutant General Rheden.

*After orders 11 at night.*

H.S.H. orders the whole army to be under arms in order of battle at one o'clock tomorrow morning. The tents are to be struck and the baggage loaded and ready to march off on the first order.

"CAMP AT HOHENOVER 18th July 1761.

"*Parole* . . .
"*Countersign* . . .
For the day to morrow Lieut. Genl. Scheill

| | | | |
|---|---|---|---|
| Major Generals | Cavalry . . . . | | Bilbow |
| | Infantry . . . . | | Townshend |
| Picquets . . | British Guards . . | | Col. Wells. |
| | „ Line . . . | | Col. Frederick |
| | Lt. Genl. Howard's Division . | | Major Oaks |
| | Prince Anhalt's . . | | „ |
| | Lt. Genl. Watgenaw's . . | | „ |

The batt. horses and baggage to return immediately, as soon therefore as the corps and regiments receive their tents they will encamp, the infantry behind their present emplacement, and the brigade of cavalry in the rear of them at a convenient distance.

Major Genl. Braum, Lieut. Col. Phillips and Major Brugmans will park their artillery in the places most suitable either in front or rear of the infantry. They are to leave their artillery that is placed in the works as they are now posted, the detachments guarding the different debouches and bridges are to remain.

The picquets of the cavalry and infantry are not to be advanced till further orders. The commanding officers are to use their utmost endeavours to prevent their men wanting bread. Should any regiment find itself in that situation or that their waggons are not arrived, they are immediately to report it to Captain Polynitz at Headquarters.

The Duke's Headquarters remain at Hohenover those of the Hereditary Prince are removed to Womble.

After Vellinghausen Prince Ferdinand tried to surprise the French near Cassel, and crossed the Diemel with that purpose; but he did not succeed, and recrossed the river, encamping at Bulme and Corbeke.

In November Prince Ferdinand made a second attempt to surprise De Broglie in his camp at Einbeck; he turned the left flank of the French, and cut off their communications with Götttingen. This obliged the French to leave their entrenched camp and retreat. After this nothing seems to have been done, and both armies went into winter quarters. The cause of the French defeat was the friction between De Broglie and Prince Soubise, divided commands, and divided counsels, for generals as well as doctors seldom agree. De Broglie wrote to his Court that Soubise delayed attacking until it was too late for De Broglie to continue it, and Soubise said that his rival began before the hour fixed, in the hopes of beating the allies without the assistance of Soubise: the old story of jealousy among officers of an equal rank—the story of the real reason of the French being driven out of the Peninsula by Wellington about fifty years after this campaign.

## 1762

Nothing was done till June in this year, and in that month Prince Ferdinand advanced again, and attacked Soubise and D'Estrees at Gravenstein, or Wilhelmstaal. The advanced guard of the allied army was formed by Lord Frederick Cavendish's brigade—11th Foot, 33rd, 51st, and Royal Welsh Fusiliers.

The attack of the allies appears to have been well combined, the French being completely surprised, the attack succeeding at all points. The Marquess of Granby's corps fell on the left wing of the French, and after a short resistance the enemy retreated, abandoning their baggage, but the retirement was well covered by De Stainville's corps, who showed himself to be an excellent rear-guard commander. Two guns, six colours, and one standard were taken by us, the total loss of the allies being 796 killed and wounded.

The name "Wilhelmstaal" appears only, as far as I can see in the *Army List*, on the colours of the 5th Fusiliers, although the above-named regiments of Lord Frederick Cavendish's brigade were present, and also a brigade of Foot Guards. In the brigade with the 5th I find the following regiments were also present: the 24th, 37th, and 12th. Lieut.-Colonel Henry Townshend, of the 1st Foot Guards, was killed in this battle; he was a cousin of George Townshend's, being the second son of the Honourable Thomas Townshend, uncle of the subject of this book. The elder brother of Colonel Henry Townshend was afterwards created Viscount Sydney.

# Minden, 1759
By James Grant

From such disasters as that at St. Cas, and the subsequent one by the shore of Lake Champlain, we gladly turn to the glories that were won by the British infantry on the plains of Minden in the following year.

Early in the spring of 1759, operations were commenced in Germany, and the Allies gained some advantage; but when the French forces were assembled they possessed so great a superiority in numbers that Prince Ferdinand was obliged to fall back as they advanced. A series of retrograde movements brought the Allied Army to the vicinity of Minden, situated on the bank of the Weser, in Westphalia.

The French Army, commanded by the Marshal de Contades, took possession of Minden, and occupied a strong position near that city, which in ancient times had been the favourite residence of several of the early German emperors.

Prince Ferdinand of Brunswick, who commanded the Allies, manoeuvred. He detached one body of troops under his nephew, the hereditary prince, and appeared to leave another exposed to the attack of the whole opposing army. Hence the destruction of this corps was resolved upon by the French commander, who put his whole army in motion for that purpose. While the French were on the march, Prince Ferdinand advanced with the allied army; and early on the morning of the 1st of August, as the leading column of the enemy attained the summit of an eminence, it was surprised to discover, instead of a few weak corps, the whole allied army formed in order of battle, in two long lines, with a reserve.

Thus, the French marshal suddenly found himself compelled to fight upon unfavourable ground; and after some delay he began to form his columns in line to the front. Some authorities make the

French 60,000 strong, and the Allies only 34,000; but Prince Ferdinand had in the field 86 battalions and no squadrons. Of these, 12 battalions and 28 squadrons were British troops, with forty-eight twelve-pound guns and four mortars.

The right of the first line was led by Lord George Sackville, and the left by the Prince of Holstein.

The centre of the second line was led by General Sporken; the right wing by the famous Marquis of Granby, the left by General Imhoff; while Major-General Prince Charles of Bevern led the corps de reserve, consisting of the Black Hussars, under Colonel Redhaezle, the Hessian Militia, the Hanoverian Hunters, the volunteers of Prussia, and other mixed corps.

The morning of Minden is recorded as having been one of great beauty; and the dense old forests that cast their shadows on the Weser, the watery barrier which the French had undertaken to defend, and which the Allies were to force at all risks, were in the fullest foliage of summer.

The allied army was formed on the plain called Todtenhausen, in front of the town of Minden, which occupies the left bank of the Weser; and the embattled walls and Gothic spires of which, the Catholic and the Lutheran, could be seen shining in the morning sun as the troops advanced. In Minden, there was a strong French garrison, the guns of which commanded its famous bridge, 600 yards in length.

At five in the morning the battle began. The 23rd Fusiliers, under the command of Lieutenant-Colonel Edward Sacheverel Pole, with the 12th and 37th British regiments, followed by Wolfe's old corps, the 20th, the Edinburgh, and 51st, under Major-Generals Waldegrave and Kingsley, flanked by two battalions of Hanoverian Guards, and the Hanoverian corps of Hardenberg, supported by three regiments of Hanoverians and one of Hessian Foot Guards, advanced with great boldness and rapidity to attack the left wing of the French army, where Marshal de Contades had posted the élite of his cavalry—the *Carbineers*, the *Gensdarmes*, and the Black and Grey *Mousquetaires*—under the queen's brother. Prince Xavier of Saxony, leader of the Household Cavalry of France.

In their advance these regiments were covered by a fire from the British artillery, which was admirably served by Captains Phillips, Macbean, Drummond, and Foy. On the other hand, the guns of the enemy opened a tremendous fire, which rent terrible chasms in the brigades of Waldegrave and Kingsley; while the *Carbineers* and

*Mousquetaires Gris* et *Rouges*, so well-known for the splendour of their costume and their headlong valour, come on with great éclat to the charge, with their accustomed fury; but a rolling volley met them as they came on. Men and horses fell over each other in hundreds. The survivors reined up in confusion and uproar, wheeled round, and galloped to the rear, their artillery recommencing its fire as the repulsed squadrons withdrew. The Hanoverian Brigade now formed up on the left of the 12th, 23rd, and 37th, and the three other British regiments on the right.

This formation was barely completed when another line of French cavalry, in gorgeous uniforms and in great strength, came rapidly forward, with all their brandished swords flashing in the sun, and with loud defiant cries; but, the *Records of the 23rd*, says:

> They were struck in mid-onset by a tempest of bullets from the British regiments, broken, and driven back with severe loss.

Pressing on again with growing ardour, the three united brigades became suddenly exposed to a fire from infantry on their flanks, but nothing could stop them. Encouraged by past success, and confident in their own prowess, they followed up their advantage, and fairly drove the boasted cavalry of France out of the field. To quote the *Campaigns of Prince Ferdinand of Brunswick*;

> Notwithstanding the loss they sustained before they could get up to the enemy, notwithstanding the repeated attacks of the enemy's cavalry; notwithstanding a fire of musketry well kept up by the enemy's infantry; notwithstanding their being exposed in front and flank; such was the unshaken firmness of those troops that nothing could stop them, and the whole body of French cavalry was routed.

The brunt of the battle was unquestionably sustained by these six noble regiments of British infantry and the two of Hanoverians. After repulsing the cavalry, they were next opposed by a column of Swiss, with whom they exchanged several thundering volleys at twenty yards' distance; but shoulder to shoulder they stood, closing in from the flanks as the dead and dying fell, the rear rank filling up the gaps in front, and never pausing in their fire save to wipe their pans, renew their priming, or change their flints.

The French now brought up several *batardes*, as they termed their eight-pounders; and the range of these extended to the cavalry of the second line, on the extreme right of which were the 3rd Dragoon Guards, 10th Dragoons, and the Scots Greys led by the aged Colonel Preston, who had been their kettle-drummer in the wars of Queen Anne, and still wore a buff coat—the last ever seen in the service.

The Swiss, who were formed in two brigades, were quickly broken and dispersed. A body of Saxons next made a show of coming down upon the conquering British infantry, but they were soon put to flight; and the brigades of Waldegrave and Kingsley continued their splendid advance, in spite of all opposition.

The aim of the French Marshals De Contades and De Broglie was to drive in or destroy either flank of the Allies; but in this they signally failed, while a terrible slaughter was made of their men.

On the left the Hessian and Hanoverian cavalry, with some regiments of Holstein and Prussian dragoons, performed good service, as also did the artillery, under the Grand Master the Count de Bukebourg, compelling the enemy to make a precipitate retreat, which speedily became general along the whole line.

The cavalry of the right had no proper opportunity given them for engaging. Smollett says:

> They were destined to support the infantry of the third line. They consisted of the British and Hanoverian horse, commanded by Lord George Sackville, whose second was the Marquis of Granby. They were posted at a considerable distance from the first line of infantry, and divided from it by a scanty wood that bordered on a heath.

It was at the instant the whole French left gave way, and the flight along the line became general, according to another historian, that:

> Prince Ferdinand of Brunswick sent orders to Lord George Sackville to advance to the charge. If these orders had been cheerfully obeyed, the battle of Minden would have been as that of Blenheim; the French Army would have been utterly destroyed, or totally routed and driven out of Germany. But whatever was the cause, the orders were not sufficiently precise, were misinterpreted, or imperfectly understood.

For this miscarriage, Lord George Sackville, after being victimised by the public press, had to appear before a general court-martial. By ten o'clock, after five hours of incessant firing, the whole French Army literally fled in the greatest disorder, with the loss of forty-three pieces of cannon, ten stand of colours, and seven standards.

On the field there lay 1,394 officers and men of the six British infantry regiments alone. The loss of the French was immense, between six and seven thousand. The Prince de Camille was among the slain, together with the Prince de Chimai and M. de la Fayette, colonels of the Grenadiers of France; and among those taken were the Count de Lutzelbourg, and the Marquis de Monti, two *marechaux de camp,* Colonel de Vogue, and many others. The rather obscure and now suppressed *Memoirs of Sir James Campbell of Ardkinlass*, who rode on Prince Ferdinand's staff that day, and who died at Edinburgh so lately as 1836, among the slain enumerates Prince Xavier of Saxony and the colonel of the *Mousquetaires Gris*, whose body he saw lying naked on the ground.

The passage of the fugitives across the Weser was a scene of unexampled horror. Beside the stone bridge already mentioned, their engineers had chained two pontoons, which broke in succession under the weight of the crowding passers; thus, many wagons full of wounded officers were swept away by the current, and the flower of the cavalry, the Carbineers and Mousquetaires, were almost destroyed; and amid their shrieks and cries were heard the exulting hurrahs and scattered shots of the advancing Allies.

The town of Minden surrendered, with 5,000 men, one-half of whom were wounded. The light troop of the Scots Greys, with some Prussian hussars, remained on the field, to protect the wounded from "death-hunters," and oversee the working parties of 2,000 peasants who buried the dead; while all the rest of the cavalry went in pursuit of the foe, and on this duty none was so active as the aged colonel of the Greys, who actually took his regiment 200 miles from the scene of the battle, and captured a vast number of prisoners. Part of the military chest, with all the splendid equipages of the Prince of Condé and Marshal de Contades, fell into his hands. An officer who served under him records that at the capture of Zerenburg old Preston received more than a dozen sword-cuts, which fell harmlessly on "his buff jerkin."

In the General Orders of the following day, it was stated that His Serene Highness desired his greatest thanks to be given to the whole army for their bravery, particularly to the British infantry and the two battalions of the Hanoverian Guards. His Serene Highness also declared publicly that, next to God, he attributed the glory of the day to the intrepidity and extraordinary behaviour of the troops.

The British regiments had the king's authority to bear on their colours the word "Minden," and in the third corner thereof the White Horse, which is still borne on the royal shield of Hanover, the badge alike of the Old Saxons in Germany, as it was of those in Kent in the earliest ages of English history.

From Minden, the Allies followed the retreating army with great energy; ascending precipices, passing morasses, overcoming many difficulties, and with so much resolution, that several French corps were nearly annihilated, and many prisoners, with a vast quantity of baggage and other plunder, taken.

Sir James Campbell says

> At Minden, a sergeant of the 51st, who had served in the wars in Flanders, made me observe on the day after the battle, when the dead bodies were stripped by the ruthless followers of the army, that the places might be distinguished where the troops of different nations had fought, by the colours and complexions of the native dead; the French in general being brown, the English and Germans fairer. This old sergeant at the same time pointed out to me several heaps of corn, which had been pulled up for the purpose of covering some object underneath.
>
> He told me it was a practice with the French soldiers, that when one of their comrades fell from a severe wound, in a field of grain, they immediately pulled and covered him over with part of it; and, to convince me of the truth of what he said, he took up a man's arm which was lying near to one of these heaps, observing that probably it belonged to the person underneath. His conjecture proved to be correct, for on uncovering the heap, we found a miserable object in the agonies of death, and beyond the reach of any human assistance.

## ALSO FROM LEONAUR
### AVAILABLE IN SOFTCOVER OR HARDCOVER WITH DUST JACKET

**THE FALL OF THE MOGHUL EMPIRE OF HINDUSTAN** *by H. G. Keene*—By the beginning of the nineteenth century, as British and Indian armies under Lake and Wellesley dominated the scene, a little over half a century of conflict brought the Moghul Empire to its knees.

**LADY SALE'S AFGHANISTAN** *by Florentia Sale*—An Indomitable Victorian Lady's Account of the Retreat from Kabul During the First Afghan War.

**THE CAMPAIGN OF MAGENTA AND SOLFERINO 1859** *by Harold Carmichael Wylly*—The Decisive Conflict for the Unification of Italy.

**FRENCH'S CAVALRY CAMPAIGN** *by J. G. Maydon*—A Special Correspondent's View of British Army Mounted Troops During the Boer War.

**CAVALRY AT WATERLOO** *by Sir Evelyn Wood*—British Mounted Troops During the Campaign of 1815.

**THE SUBALTERN** *by George Robert Gleig*—The Experiences of an Officer of the 85th Light Infantry During the Peninsular War.

**NAPOLEON AT BAY, 1814** *by F. Loraine Petre*—The Campaigns to the Fall of the First Empire.

**NAPOLEON AND THE CAMPAIGN OF 1806** *by Colonel Vachée*—The Napoleonic Method of Organisation and Command to the Battles of Jena & Auerstädt.

**THE COMPLETE ADVENTURES IN THE CONNAUGHT RANGERS** *by William Grattan*—The 88th Regiment during the Napoleonic Wars by a Serving Officer.

**BUGLER AND OFFICER OF THE RIFLES** *by William Green & Harry Smith*—With the 95th (Rifles) during the Peninsular & Waterloo Campaigns of the Napoleonic Wars.

**NAPOLEONIC WAR STORIES** *by Sir Arthur Quiller-Couch*—Tales of soldiers, spies, battles & sieges from the Peninsular & Waterloo campaingns.

**CAPTAIN OF THE 95TH (RIFLES)** *by Jonathan Leach*—An officer of Wellington's sharpshooters during the Peninsular, South of France and Waterloo campaigns of the Napoleonic wars.

**RIFLEMAN COSTELLO** *by Edward Costello*—The adventures of a soldier of the 95th (Rifles) in the Peninsular & Waterloo Campaigns of the Napoleonic wars.

AVAILABLE ONLINE AT **www.leonaur.com**
AND FROM ALL GOOD BOOK STORES

# ALSO FROM LEONAUR
## AVAILABLE IN SOFTCOVER OR HARDCOVER WITH DUST JACKET

**ZULU:1879** *by D.C.F. Moodie & the Leonaur Editors*—The Anglo-Zulu War of 1879 from contemporary sources: First Hand Accounts, Interviews, Dispatches, Official Documents & Newspaper Reports.

**THE RED DRAGOON** *by W.J. Adams*—With the 7th Dragoon Guards in the Cape of Good Hope against the Boers & the Kaffir tribes during the 'war of the axe' 1843-48'.

**THE RECOLLECTIONS OF SKINNER OF SKINNER'S HORSE** *by James Skinner*—James Skinner and his 'Yellow Boys' Irregular cavalry in the wars of India between the British, Mahratta, Rajput, Mogul, Sikh & Pindarree Forces.

**A CAVALRY OFFICER DURING THE SEPOY REVOLT** *by A. R. D. Mackenzie*—Experiences with the 3rd Bengal Light Cavalry, the Guides and Sikh Irregular Cavalry from the outbreak to Delhi and Lucknow.

**A NORFOLK SOLDIER IN THE FIRST SIKH WAR** *by J W Baldwin*—Experiences of a private of H.M. 9th Regiment of Foot in the battles for the Punjab, India 1845-6.

**TOMMY ATKINS' WAR STORIES: 14 FIRST HAND ACCOUNTS**—Fourteen first hand accounts from the ranks of the British Army during Queen Victoria's Empire.

**THE WATERLOO LETTERS** *by H. T. Siborne*—Accounts of the Battle by British Officers for its Foremost Historian.

**NEY: GENERAL OF CAVALRY VOLUME 1—1769-1799** *by Antoine Bulos*—The Early Career of a Marshal of the First Empire.

**NEY: MARSHAL OF FRANCE VOLUME 2—1799-1805** *by Antoine Bulos*—The Early Career of a Marshal of the First Empire.

**AIDE-DE-CAMP TO NAPOLEON** *by Philippe-Paul de Ségur*—For anyone interested in the Napoleonic Wars this book, written by one who was intimate with the strategies and machinations of the Emperor, will be essential reading.

**TWILIGHT OF EMPIRE** *by Sir Thomas Ussher & Sir George Cockburn*—Two accounts of Napoleon's Journeys in Exile to Elba and St. Helena: Narrative of Events by Sir Thomas Ussher & Napoleon's Last Voyage: Extract of a diary by Sir George Cockburn.

**PRIVATE WHEELER** *by William Wheeler*—The letters of a soldier of the 51st Light Infantry during the Peninsular War & at Waterloo.

AVAILABLE ONLINE AT www.leonaur.com
AND FROM ALL GOOD BOOK STORES

www.ingramcontent.com/pod-product-compliance
Lightning Source LLC
Chambersburg PA
CBHW021007090426
42738CB00007B/692